Praise for *Preaching Jesus*

"Eunjoo Mary Kim's book stands as an eminent contribution to the fields of preaching theology and methodology, providing a postcolonial lens through which to explore Christology. This perspective serves as a supplement to the diverse portrayals of Christ found in the Synoptic Gospels, the Gospel of John, and other New Testament Scriptures. Positioned within the rich context of literature on postcolonial and Jesus-centered preaching, this invaluable study conducts a critical examination of past sermons on Christology within preaching arenas. Moreover, it meticulously scrutinizes current sermon discourses and presents insights for the future, introducing alternative and re-imagined approaches."—**Namjoong Kim**, associate professor of the practice of ministry, director of the Korean Doctoral Program, Claremont School of Theology

"This decolonizing feminist approach to Christology promises to be of signal importance for homiletics and pastoral theology. Kim's intersectionally rich book invites us to imagine Jesus beyond the constraints and distortions of traditional Western theology. Key postcolonial concepts—the conflicts and complicities of the hybrid self, the violence of nativist rhetoric, and more—are illuminated in these pages. Kim urges preachers to craft a dialogical space in which subversive truth-telling and solidarity can honor those whose experience has been commodified or disfigured by colonizing practices. This fresh reframing of homiletical theology will spur lively conversations in homiletics classrooms for years to come."—**Carolyn J. Sharp**, professor of homiletics, Yale Divinity School

"*Preaching Jesus* is a wonderful addition to the recent efforts that have been made to bring homiletics and postcolonial studies into conversation with each other. It delves into Christological themes from postcolonial perspectives where Jesus is featured as boundary-breaker, boundary-connector, and boundary-transcender. Readers are invited to celebrate the liturgical season of Lent, Easter, Advent, and Christmas, while exploring through preaching particular texts of the Gospels of John, Luke, and Matthew."—**HyeRan Kim-Cragg**, Timothy Eaton Memorial Church Professor of Preaching, Emmanuel College

"Kim invites readers into a transformative vision, where the story of Jesus is reimagined through a postcolonial lens, challenging traditional interpretations and fostering a global dialogue for healing and unity."—**Rev. Sunggu A. Yang**, associate professor of theology and Christian ministries, director of the Margaret Fell Scholars Program, George Fox University

Preaching Jesus

Preaching Jesus
Postcolonial Approaches

Eunjoo Mary Kim

ROWMAN & LITTLEFIELD
Lanham • Boulder • New York • London

Published by Rowman & Littlefield
An imprint of The Rowman & Littlefield Publishing Group, Inc.
4501 Forbes Boulevard, Suite 200, Lanham, Maryland 20706
www.rowman.com
86-90 Paul Street, London EC2A 4NE

Copyright © 2024 by The Rowman & Littlefield Publishing Group, Inc.

All rights reserved. No part of this book may be reproduced in any form or by any electronic or mechanical means, including information storage and retrieval systems, without written permission from the publisher, except by a reviewer who may quote passages in a review.

British Library Cataloguing in Publication Information Available

Library of Congress Cataloging-in-Publication Data
978-1-5381-9205-4 (cloth)
978-1-5381-9206-1 (paperback)
978-1-5381-9207-8 (electronic)

For my husband Joseph S. Lee—
my Lover, Best Friend, and Forever Cheerleader

Contents

Preface xi

CHAPTER 1: Preaching Jesus as Postcolonial Self 1
CHAPTER 2: Preaching Jesus as Postcolonial Song 21
CHAPTER 3: Preaching Jesus as Postcolonial Child 41
CHAPTER 4: Preaching Jesus as Postcolonial Body 59
CHAPTER 5: Preaching Jesus as Postcolonial Friend. 79
Sermon: A Letter to Mary and Elizabeth (Luke 1:39–45) . 101

Notes. 109
Bibliography 123
Index 131
About the Author 143

Preface

This book grew out of the 2022 Beecher Lectures at Yale Divinity School. The first three chapters are expansions of three lectures on the subject of "Preaching Jesus: Postcolonial Approaches," while the last two are additions to that theme. The five chapters engage in conversation around the question, "What would it be like to preach Jesus from a postcolonial perspective?" These chapters invite readers to explore fresh theological meanings of the Christological event and to investigate hermeneutical and homiletical methods effective in preaching Jesus in our neo- and postcolonial world. My gratitude to Gregory Sterling, Dean of Yale Divinity School, goes beyond words for his invitation to the lectureship. I am also grateful to the Louisville Institute for their Sabbatical Research Grant and to Vanderbilt Divinity School for granting me sabbatical leave over the 2022–23 academic year. With this generous support, I was able to complete this volume, which seeks to offer a unique postcolonial voice on preaching Jesus.

What does it mean to preach Jesus? For Christian preachers, Jesus is the central theme and heart of their sermons, and as a subject, can never be exhausted. Answers to the question may be as diverse as preachers' spiritual and cultural experiences, denominational upbringing, and ministerial training. Above all, their answers will vary depending on the way they understand who and what Jesus is for themselves and for their communities. Homiletical resources about what and how to preach about Jesus also vary according to different theological points of view. However, it is hard to find books from a postcolonial perspective aimed at helping preachers preach Jesus, even though this is one of the most helpful critical lenses through which to see and preach the good news in today's complex neo- and postcolonial context.

We live in a globalized, multicultural world—a consequence of colonialism and neocolonialism—where we are increasingly aware of the tensions and conflicts caused by racism, sexism, culture and religious imperialism, and the economic disparity between the colonized and the colonizers, both past and present. The compelling task for Christian preaching is thus to nurture the gift of difference and solidarity across racial, gender, cultural, and class boundaries so that there might be reconciliation between these groups. Postcolonial theory promises a new framework for today's preachers, that they might preach Jesus as an act of transforming the world. This theory helps preachers examine the root causes of the interwoven social and ethical problems that have resulted from a long history of imperial colonialism. Postcolonial theory also provides preachers with new approaches to reading the Christological Event in the Bible, in order to preach relevant messages for the common good of both colonized and colonizers.

Currently, there are two books on the subject of postcolonial homiletics—Sarah Travis's *Decolonizing Preaching: The Pulpit as Postcolonial Space* and HyeRan Kim-Cragg's *Postcolonial Preaching: Creating a Ripple Effect*.[1] While these books render essential information and knowledge about postcolonial preaching, this present work offers a unique contribution to the field of homiletics because it takes a postcolonial perspective as its point of departure for preaching Jesus. Here, Christological themes are explored from a postcolonial perspective, and readers are encouraged to reimagine the identity of Jesus by creatively employing diverse postcolonial hermeneutical approaches. This work also offers fresh theological insights and concrete and practical homiletical strategies that can help preachers convey a message that is more theologically appropriate and homiletically effective for contemporary listeners.

On a personal level, a postcolonial perspective reflects my own theological and homiletical journey. I spent my early life in postcolonial Korea, a country occupied for thirty-six years—though not by a Western country, but by Japan—and which then went through a chaotic and tragic postcolonial era after emancipation in 1945. The Korean War (1950 to 1953) destroyed 80 percent of the country's industrial buildings and infrastructure, leaving Korea the poorest country in the world. The war ceased only at the cost of dividing the nation into North and South, and today Korea remains the prime example of a war-ravaged country still divided in two. This national tragedy, a consequence of imperial colonialism, has caused political, socioeconomic, and military insecurity, as well as personal and collective traumas for the Korean people for more than seventy years.

Like other former colonized countries, South Korea was under a military dictatorship that, in order to maintain power, persecuted democracy movements involving innocent intellectuals and college students. On top of the political oppression, the people suffered poverty and the sacrifice of their human rights through the exploitation of their labor, under the pretext of national economic growth. During my high school and college years in the 1970s and '80s, I was distraught over this situation and despaired at the thought of a hopeless future for my country and its people. This lived experience drove me to search for hope in the Bible, and in this endeavor, I was fortunate to learn from great pioneer Korean theologians at Ewha Woman's University. These included professors Hyuk Huh, who studied Rudolf Bultmann in Germany and introduced his theology to the Korean church; Soon-Kyung Park, the first Korean Barthian, who translated Barth's *Church Dogmatics* into Korean; David Kwang-sun Suh, one of the first Minjung scholars (i.e., Korean liberation theology); and Chang Sang, the first Korean female biblical scholar.

Preface

When I came to the United States for my advanced theological education, I experienced a different reality of the postcolonial world. At Princeton Theological Seminary, I was fascinated by the in-depth teaching on Christian theology and homiletical theory. But after completing my M. Div. and Ph.D. programs, I realized that what I had learned was in fact Western theology and rhetoric. I then wondered if there were any Asian philosophies and communication theories to further deepen my understanding of Christian faith and the practice of preaching. This question led to research and consequently publishing my first monograph on homiletics, *Preaching the Presence of God: A Homiletic from an Asian American Perspective*.[2] I believe this work has contributed to the dismantling of Western cultural and intellectual imperialism in theological education and to the decolonizing of homiletical theories.

During my twenty-four years of teaching at Iliff School of Theology in Denver, Colorado, I experienced another aspect of the postcolonial world. I enjoyed my teaching and research, but I was always a guest, a member of the FOC ("the Faculty of Color"). White supremacy and Western cultural imperialism in the institution were stumbling blocks to practicing "radical hospitality" or "just hospitality," to use Letty Russell's term,[3] in which hosts and guests, or the colonizers and the colonized, live as a family of God, taking turns in serving and being served. So I challenged the church and the academy to renew their theology and practice in ways appropriate to our globalized postcolonial, multicultural world by publishing two more books, *Preaching in an Age of Globalization* and *Christian Preaching and Worship in Multicultural Contexts: A Practical Theological Approach*.[4] Moreover, my experience of sexism within and beyond the Korean American community drove me to research a history of women preachers worldwide and write *Women Preaching: Theology and Practice through the Ages*.[5] All these publications represent my postcolonial resistance, be it implicit or explicit, in my particular postcolonial context.

This book is now another act of postcolonial resistance, the outcome of my serious thought about what it really means to preach Jesus in our neo- and postcolonial world. We are all—whether formerly colonizers or colonized—the offspring of a complex history. The Christian mission and the Christian pulpit have also been influenced by Western colonialism and have proclaimed Jesus from that perspective. How then can postcolonial approaches make a difference in preaching Jesus? The many postcolonial approaches used in this book will help preachers reinterpret the stories, metaphors, and characters in the Bible and create new images of Jesus rooted in his historical identity as a colonized person. Preaching Jesus with new images that are totally different from the traditional colonial ones not only challenges listeners to reconsider their individual and communal identities as followers of Jesus but also provides them with theological and ethical guidance for living out those identities in daily life. Ultimately, preaching Jesus through postcolonial approaches is a prophetic ministry that awakens listeners and their communities to seek reconciliation between colonized and colonizers, and suggests a common engagment of faith and hope for the life-enhancing future of all people living in the twenty-first century.

It cannot be overemphasized that to make a clear-cut distinction between the colonized and the colonizer is inadequate because life situations related to race, ethnicity, gender, sexuality, and class are as diverse and complex as the world history of colonialism, postcolonialism, and neocolonialism. To speak of the colonized and the colonizer, of Western colonialism and European colonial Christianity, risks reducing the issue to mere essentialism by generalizing such diversity and complexity. However, these terms are frequently used in this book within a particular historical context or as the practice of "strategic essentialism," which is a pragmatically helpful way to speak of them when discussing important matters in each situation. As feminist theologian Joyce Ann Mercer explains, "[i]n strategic essentialism, the conscious awareness of the risk of essentializing is temporarily embraced in a strategic manner as a way to move constructively where important matters are at stake, yet always with an eye to the potential unintended consequences of these choices."[6]

There is no single methodological approach to preaching Jesus from a postcolonial perspective. The five chapters of this book employ diverse postcolonial hermeneutical and homiletical methods across a broad disciplinary spectrum. This range includes intersectional and interdisciplinary studies with historical, literary, and cultural approaches, in dialogue with phenomenological philosophy, a postcolonial practical theological method, postcolonial feminist interpretation, postcolonial biblical hermeneutics, and postcolonial intertextuality. All these approaches invite the colonized and their descendants to be conversation partners and reflect their lived experiences in reimagining the identity of Jesus. Moreover, the theological and homiletical insights gained through such postcolonial approaches will help preachers invite their listeners into a partnership with the Triune God to participate in God's reconciling work. The postcolonial approaches used in this book contest the dominance of traditional assumptions and practices of preaching Jesus and propose a new homiletical paradigm that makes it possible for Christian preaching to contribute to the transformation of our present world into a life lived together in justice and peace.

As the outset, the first chapter summarizes a variety of homiletical theories about preaching Jesus and presents him as the model of the postcolonial self, based on reading the Samaritan woman's story in John 4:4–42 from a postcolonial perspective. The second chapter explains the nature and function of a postcolonial imagination in preaching Jesus and interprets Mary's pregnancy story in Luke 1:46–55 as a postcolonial song signifying the identity of the unborn Jesus. The third chapter focuses on the issue of global migration and identifies Jesus as a postcolonial child who points to the present migrants who are victims of imperial colonialism also. This is argued from a postcolonial feminist reading of the story of Jesus' exile to Egypt in Matthew 2:13–23. The fourth chapter explores in John 20 the theological meaning of Jesus' resurrected body, complete with scars, and depicts the risen Jesus as a postcolonial body symbolizing reconciliation between colonized and colonizers. The last chapter reads Jesus' Great Commission in Matthew 28:16–20 through an intertextual approach and asserts that the risen Jesus is a postcolonial friend who invites his followers to extend his friendship to the world.

Christian preachers are constantly challenged to reinterpret the radical grace found in the events of Jesus Christ and preach prophetic messages in changing contexts. While the five chapters of this book can help with preaching the stories of Jesus from the diverse angles of a postcolonial lens, these chapters offer just a few examples of preaching Jesus in this way. Hence, this book is an open invitation to those who are serious about teaching and learning to preach Jesus from a postcolonial perspective, to write further chapters in a similar vein. In this way, they may in turn help others proclaim the good news of Jesus Christ in theologically responsible, culturally relevant, and homiletically creative ways in our neo- and postcolonial world.

Chapter 1

Preaching Jesus as Postcolonial Self

The uniqueness of Christian preaching is that it preaches Jesus in the framework of the Triune God. Churches have traditionally proclaimed Jesus as the Messiah by using lectionaries following the Christian calendar or by expositing the biographical stories of Jesus in the Gospels in their weekly sermons. While numerous resources for preaching Jesus are available in print and online, they rarely provide any critical analysis of the impact of European colonialism in the tradition of interpreting the Christological event or information about preaching Jesus from a postcolonial perspective. This first chapter establishes a groundwork for this approach by presenting a brief overview of postcolonialism and its influence on Christian theology and preaching. The first section critically examines the literature dealing with contemporary homiletic theories about preaching Jesus from this perspective, and then summarizes the development of postcolonial theology. The second section explains postcolonial homiletics, identifying its distinctive characteristics, and explores the hybrid identity of Jesus. The third section reads the story of the Samaritan woman (John 4:4–42) from a postcolonial perspective and presents a new image of Jesus as represented in this historical and cultural context. The last section provides homiletical insights into preaching Jesus as a postcolonial self.

Chapter 1

Preaching Jesus and Postcolonialism

There are presently four primary monographs concerning preaching Jesus: David Buttrick's *Preaching Jesus Christ: An Exercise in Homiletic Theology*, published in 1988; Charles Campbell's *Preaching Jesus: New Directions for Homiletics in Hans Frei's Postliberal Theology*, published in 1996; David Lose's *Preaching Jesus: Preaching in a Postmodern World*, published in 2003; and Annette Brownlee's *Preaching Jesus Christ Today: Six Questions for Moving from Scripture to Sermon*, published in 2018.[1] Each of these books is written from a distinctive theological perspective. Buttrick provides homiletical guidance from a liberal and liberational point of view, Campbell and Brownlee from a postliberal perspective, and Lose from a postmodern angle.

While each makes a unique contribution to the topic of "preaching Jesus," these books share at least three commonalities. First, they confine their audiences to members of European American, middle- and upper-middle-class Protestant churches. The authors are concerned about the decline of these mainstream Christian churches and seek to revive them through preaching the renewal of the Christian faith in Jesus Christ. The second commonality is that they all fail to engage constructively with the world in which their readers live, which is globalized, multicultural, and pluralistic. Instead, they regard their audience as racially, ethnically, and culturally homogenous, and seek to develop a univocal identity of the community, relying on common cultural, racial, and ecclesial experiences. The last common feature of these books is that they all overlook the fact that Jesus lived under the Roman Empire as one of the colonized and that his identity was that of a hybrid of the colonized Jewish culture and the imperial culture of the Empire. Moreover, they ignore the influence of Western colonialism on subsequent theology about, and proclamation of the identity of Jesus.

The hundreds of years of Western colonialism have resulted in a complex, globalized world where we are increasingly aware of differences in nationality, culture, religion, ethnicity, gender, class, and language, and in which we experience violent conflicts daily. As Roman Catholic systematic theologian Ansel Min points out, the Christian churches are compelled to provide theological and ethical guidance for living together peacefully despite our differences. In this "new *kairos* of globalization," the urgent task for Christian preaching in churches and other public spaces, in person or online, is to nurture the gift of difference and "the mutual solidarity of those who are different."[2] Perhaps ignorance of this demand is one of the reasons for the decline of the mainstream Protestant churches.

In this reality, postcolonialism is a most useful critical theory for analyzing our complex contexts for preaching, and for examining the root causes of these interwoven ethical issues. It also provides a framework for a homiletical paradigm that can facilitate preaching Jesus as an act of transformation in our globalized, neo- and postcolonial world. It may seem banal, but it is worth remembering that the frame of reference for the term "postcolonial" is Western colonial imperialism, and that the prefix "post" means not only "after" but also "having gone through." The dual meaning of "post" considers the fact that even though we live in a historical era in which Western imperialism has officially come to an end in most parts of the world, it nevertheless continues—despite the absence of colonies—in the more subtle and yet similarly brutal economic, social, cultural, and political forms of neocolonialism. Thus, as postcolonial feminist theologian Kwok Pui-lan clarifies in her book, *Postcolonial Imagination and Feminist Theology*, the term "postcolonial" denotes not merely "a temporal period or a political transition of power," but "the decolonization process" that seeks "to unmask colonial epistemological frameworks, unravel Eurocentric logics, and interrogate stereotypical cultural representations."[3] In this sense, postcoloniality is a critical consciousness of both colonial and postcolonial conditions,[4] and postcolonialism is a critical theory that serves as both deconstructive and constructive critiques of the hegemonic forces of colonial imperialism. Postcolonial theory investigates and analyzes all manner of colonial endeavors in all areas of human life, both that of the colonized and the colonizers, past and present; and it provides ethical direction for such emerging issues as economic and power disparities, religious and cultural diversity, racism and sexism, the global influx of migrants, and mounting ecological crises.

Since being planted into the soil of Christian theology and biblical studies by R. S. Sugirtharajah, Warren Carter, Kwok Pui-lan, Katherine Keller, Joerg Rieger, and other theologians during the 1990s and the early 2000s, postcolonial theology has become one of the most powerful means of re-examining the Eurocentric dominance of these fields. It has redirected theological discourse from white, middle-class Eurocentric norms to those of the colonized, focusing on themes such as hybrid identity, interdependence, and border-crossing between races, religions, genders, and so on. Postcolonial theology tends to be regarded as one of the liberation theologies, or a "supplement to the liberation tradition,"[5] because, like other liberation theologies, it identifies our social location in terms of power relations between the oppressed and the oppressors. Moreover, like other liberation theologies, postcolonial theology has a commitment to the narratives of oppressed people as an important basis for social ethics, and it grants epistemological priority to their experiences. In other words, it shares with other liberation theologies the preferential love for a particular group of the oppressed—here the victims of Western colonial and neocolonial imperialism.

However, postcolonial theology is distinguished from other liberation theologies by at least three distinctive characteristics: First, the major critical tool is cultural studies. Like other liberational theologies, postcolonial theology is concerned with the various forms of oppression, such as racism, sexism, economic disparity, and political persecution. Yet, through the critical cultural analysis of postcolonial conditions, it recognizes that Western cultural imperialism grounded in white supremacy and Western cultural superiority intersects with other oppressive powers and contributes to systemic injustice and the marginalization of the colonized. Thus, a task of postcolonial theology is to decolonize Western cultural imperialism dominating our world.

The second characteristic of postcolonial theology is that it integrates all liberation theologies into one theological claim. As Kwok rightly stresses, there is no single postcolonial theology, since "the experiences of colonialism are far from homogeneous."[6] Hence the approach is comprehensive and multifaceted, with diverse theological concerns, including particular concerns of feminist theology, Black theology, and other liberation theologies. In other words, the subject matter of the various liberation theologies can be probed from a postcolonial perspective without denying the importance of their particularities.

The third distinctive characteristic of postcolonial theology is that it does not accept a binary between the colonizing oppressors and the colonized oppressed. The reality of our globalized postcolonial world is too complex and ambiguous to make such clear-cut distinctions. Everyone coexists in the complexity of postcolonial conditions without geographical and cultural boundaries. And everyone's experiences are so diverse that territorial, cultural, and racial essentialism is inappropriate. Thus, as feminist theologian Letty Russell states in her posthumously published book, *Just Hospitality: God's Welcome in a World of Difference*, "whether colonizer or colonized, we are all postcolonial subjects continually affected by the history and ongoing economic, religious, cultural, and political implications of colonialism, albeit in very different ways."[7] In this situation, instead of "the dualistic paradigm of oppressor/oppressed"[8] or colonizer/colonized, postcolonial theology aims to create an "in-between space" or a "third space" where we seek the way of solidarity with each other. Such a theology encourages both colonized and colonizers to dismantle the white supremacy in their cultural and religious identities, and invites them into a third space of self-reflection, where they can critically examine their connections to Western colonial imperialism. Here, it is noteworthy that Andrew Wymer, a European American homiletician, identifies the white postcolonial preacher as "a race traitor" who is "nominally classified as white, but who defies the rules of whiteness so flagrantly as to jeopardize his or her ability to draw upon the privileges of white skin."[9]

POSTCOLONIAL HOMILETICS AND THE HYBRID IDENTITY

These three distinctive characteristics of postcolonial theology help redirect homiletical theory and practice. Historically, there has been no precolonial theory of homiletics since St. Augustine's *De Doctrina Christiana*, Book IV, was published in 427 AD as the first homiletics textbook.[10] Thus, from the fifth century under the Roman Empire through successive periods of European domination, Western Christian homiletics evolved to accommodate European imperial culture. Throughout this influential Christian period, the identity of Jesus Christ has been colonized, with Jesus portrayed as white, and with the Christian calendar and liturgical colors representing Western cultural elements. Moreover, Christian preaching has been complicit in helping European colonialism worldwide, by proclaiming the colonizers' image of the whiteness of Jesus Christ and ignoring the fact that the historical Jesus was a colonized Jew within the Roman Empire. The four aforementioned books on preaching Jesus are examples of Western imperial homiletics, in the sense that they overlook the negative influence of European Christian colonialism on the process of interpreting the Christological event in the Scriptures and in rhetorical approaches to preaching Jesus.

In 2014, Sarah Travis, a European Canadian homiletician, made a remarkable contribution to homiletics with her book, *Decolonizing Preaching: The Pulpit as Postcolonial Space*.[11] Assuming her primary readership is European Christian descendants, she defines postcolonial preaching as participation in the process of decolonizing the listeners' minds.[12] She perceives colonialism and imperialism as an ongoing reality in our time and place, and believes that we can change the way we preach by changing the way we engage with Scripture. That is, by discovering "new language and images to replace what is familiar and comfortable,"[13] preachers can proclaim "a gospel that transcends and transforms discourses of power."[14]

The following year, 2015, the journal *Homiletic* devoted a special issue to postcolonial preaching. Its five articles elaborated and expanded on the theories of postcolonial preaching that Travis had initiated. Four years after that, in 2019, the Academy of Homiletics brought postcolonialism into live discussion by choosing "Unmasking Whiteness" as its conference theme. Many of the conference papers carefully examined the history and practice of Christian preaching. They explored the long-standing homiletical legacy of white preaching, and then proposed deconstructing this racialized domination in homiletics.[15] And further, in 2021, Asian-Canadian practical theologian HyeRan Kim-Cragg published her book, *Postcolonial Preaching: Creating a Ripple Effect*, in which she suggests that present-day preaching should address those historic concerns gently but persistently, and in so doing, change our way of living by means of effective homiletical strategies.[16]

With multiple voices, resources have enriched postcolonial discourse in the field of homiletics with multiple voices. Following suit, I define postcolonial homiletics as a set of theories that dismantle traditional ideas and practices of preaching embedded in European colonial Christianity, thereby making it possible to preach "postcolonially" with a new and expanded imagination. Postcolonial preaching is not only about decolonizing the pulpit; it is also about refurbishing it with fresh images, metaphors, and stories of the Triune God, through which Christian identity is renewed and the Christian church revitalized.

One crucial task of postcolonial preaching is to retrieve the identity of Jesus from a usurped and skewed perspective, thereby enabling the concept of "hybridity" to more fully flesh out and present Jesus in a new way. Hybridity in postcolonial theory refers to the genetic and cultural mix that results from colonial imperialism. As Catherine Keller explains, the hybrid identity of previously or presently colonized peoples is a product of the colonizers' direct invasion, violation, and rape, or of the indirect subjection of the colonized that has stimulated survivalist strategies of mimicry and appropriation.[17] Postcolonial theory, on the one hand, recognizes hybridity negatively as a location of conflict, hostility, ambiguity, and confusion, and as a site for resistance. On the other hand, as Homi Bhabha and other postcolonial critics affirm, hybridity has possibilities for creativity. In *The Location of Culture*, Bhabha contends that "the meaning and symbols of culture have no primordial unity or fixity,"[18] and he challenges the binary logic of modern identity politics. For Bhabha, identity is not "a homogenizing, unifying force,"[19] but a product of cultural hybridity. Edward Said, a postcolonial literary and cultural critic, also attests that every cultural form and cultural experience is "radically, quintessentially hybrid."[20] He explains:

> No one today is purely *one* thing. Labels like Indian, or woman, or Muslim, or American are not more than starting-points, which if followed into actual experience for only a moment are quickly left behind. . . . Survival [in this reality] is about the connections between things . . . [by thinking] concretely, and sympathetically, contrapuntally, about others [rather] than only about "us."[21]

Along with Said, Bhabha regards hybridity as an unavoidable reality of human life and calls this productive capacity a "Third Space."[22] In his view, the third space is something like "the *inbetween* space that carries the burden of the meaning of culture,"[23] in which marginalized ethnic minorities, such as oppressed, immigrant, and colonized people, are "interstitial" agents who resist the dominant culture of society and embrace the creative space of their in-betweenness, in between the dominant culture and their marginalized one. In that third space, they construct a hybrid culture and identity integral to themselves through the "negotiation" and "translation" of their cultural identities between the two cultures. Their culturally hybrid identity is distinct from both; it is neither one of them. It is something new that provides them with a fresh perception of who and what they are.[24]

In some senses, the postcolonial concept of hybridity corresponds to the postmodern concept of deconstruction. Deconstruction is an ongoing process of overturning the established basis of meaning or fixed categories of understanding. It is also a process of creating space by challenging assumptions and opening the field of inquiry to other voices. For example, Jacques Derrida, Michel Foucault, Julia Kristeva, and others point to the cultural power dynamic at work in Western ontology that assumes "being" as "changelessness" and reduces "alterity and difference to a unifying sameness."[25] They argue that these ontological assumptions backing modern grand narratives and ideologies should be deconstructed from the recognition of the importance of cultural difference and diversity.

Yet, the postmodern concept of deconstruction is Eurocentric in its conceptual thrust. As practical theologian Tom Beaudoin criticizes, postmodern theologies seldom question "the continuing effect of the history of white supremacy, evidenced by the bias (in many strands of postmodern theologies) toward Western (and especially Continental-derived), white, European-identified philosophical thinkers."[26] He further argues that

> [w]hile diversity in race and ethnicity, as well as interracial and interethnic identification, found increasing acceptance, it was not a regular focus of postmodern cultural description. Despite

the gains of postmodern theological explorations, it also appears that the theological turn to the postmodern was a way that formerly privileged cultural actors, including theologians and pastoral workers, mourned lost hegemony.... Postmodern theologies can even, ironically, perpetuate forms of "hegemony masquerading under the guise of cultural heterogeneity."[27]

While the postmodern cultural approach represents predominantly Eurocentric voices, the postcolonial approach to cultural hybridity is concerned with voices from the four corners of the globe where the colonized, diasporic intellectuals, and conscientized colonizers and their descendants all critically reflect on the negative impacts of Western colonial and neocolonial cultures. Postcolonial theologians and preachers understand that it is a mistake to see the colonialists' interests and values as universal. They question the Eurocentric beliefs and values dominating the process of meaning-making around Christian texts and deconstruct prescribed ways of reading them. They not only evaluate Western theology and biblical interpretation critically, but also attempt to create new hybrid cultural images of Jesus to help listeners acquire "a new identity" as the followers of Jesus.

Understanding the relation between cultural hybridity and the formation of a new identity can be deepened through a critical conversation with French philosopher Paul Ricoeur. Like postmodernists and postcolonial critics, Ricoeur disagrees with the modern construction of being as changelessness or a unifying sameness. Yet, his uniqueness is his hermeneutical approach to the open-endedness of the self through dialectical interactions with others, or to use the postcolonial term, the hybridity of the self. In *Oneself as Another*, Ricoeur proposes "a hermeneutics of the self" that focuses on the narrative identity of the self that is involved in plot and character.[28] He elaborates that the investigation of "Who?" directly relates to such questions as "Who is speaking of what? Who does what? About whom and about what does one construct a narrative? Who is morally responsible for what?"[29] These questions guide recognition of the identity of the character in the narrative and link the question "Who?" to the question "What?" In other words, the identity of the character ("Who?") is defined by his or her role ("What?") in the story and is recognized by the other who speaks of it. Thus, Ricoeur states that "one cannot be thought of without the other"[30] because "the *self* is implied reflexively in the operations, the analysis of which precedes the return toward this self."[31]

While Ricoeur's philosophical and hermeneutical discourse on the self provides common ground with a postcolonial concept of the hybrid self, which is open to the other, the problem with Ricoeur is that his philosophical roots in Heideggerian existential ontology and Husserl's philosophical phenomenology make his use of the term "otherness" abstract and speculative. Although he discusses the complexity of otherness, or "the polysemy of otherness,"[32] and stresses that the self is essentially opening onto the world, he does not elaborate on what kind of world he refers to, and who belongs to his "metacategory of otherness."[33] People experience the world differently in their particular sociopolitical, economic, religious, and cultural settings, and the postcolonial approach takes this difference seriously, particularly the otherness of those who have been marginalized by colonialism and neocolonialism. It is questionable if Ricoeur counts racially different people who have been colonized by France and other Western countries in his metacategory of otherness.

The postcolonial concept of hybridity that characterizes the postcolonial identity of the self is open to the otherness of the experiences of the colonized and their recognitions. A pivotal concern of postcolonial preaching is to help listeners be open to otherness, so that they might reconfigure their Christian identity as postcolonial selves and live it out as agents, thereby transforming our society, locally and globally. Thus, one task of the Christian preacher is to search for a prototype of the postcolonial self in the Bible and other sacred texts.

Jesus as Postcolonial Self

One biblical text that presents the image of the postcolonial self is the story of the Samaritan woman in John 4:5–42. It is the Gospel lesson for the Third Sunday of Lent in Year A in the *Revised Common Lectionary*. Lent was originally observed in Rome from around 330 CE as the season for the final preparation of those who were to be baptized at Easter.[34] It was a time to reflect on a new identity, i.e., what it means to be a member of the Christian church in the love of Jesus Christ. However, Lent gradually developed into a time for public exercises of penance. This shift of emphasis from preparation for baptism to public penitential observance is demonstrated by the imposition of ashes on Ash Wednesday, which is the first day of Lent.[35] Reading the story of the Samaritan woman as a story of identity formation revives the original meaning of Lent.

The story of the Samaritan woman is divided into three sections—the conversation between Jesus and the Samaritan woman (vv. 4–26), the work of the Samaritan woman as an active agent (vv. 27–30, 39–42), and the conversation between Jesus and his disciples (vv. 31–38). Traditionally, this text has been interpreted as the story of the salvation of a woman who is inferior, allowing her to understand what Jesus says, and the immorality in her personal life. Jesus, by contrast, is presented as a model of the ideal patriarch with authority in terms of individual morality and sageness. However, the perspective of liberation theology focuses instead on the image of Jesus as a liberator who sets the woman free from sociocultural and religious oppression, while feminist theology elevates the woman's status to that of a theologian who freely holds a long, profound theological conversation with Jesus.[36]

It is also noteworthy that postcolonial biblical theologian Musa W. Dube reads this story as an imperializing "mission narrative," in which Jesus and his disciples proselytize Samaritans by embracing the ideology of imperial expansion.[37] In the story, according to Dube, patriarchy and imperialism are intertwined, and the Samaritan woman is characterized as an "ignorant native" who is "morally and religiously lacking something," while Jesus is the "superior traveler" who is "knowledgeable" and "powerful."[38] Dube insists that the Samaritan woman's story should be rewritten for decolonization and the empowerment of women. She points to a decolonizing reading of the story found in Botswanan Mositi Torontle's novel, *The Victims*,[39] as an example. In Torontle's story, recreated against the historical background of the apartheid of southern Africa, a Botswanan woman meets another woman dressed in white clothing, rather than a male white Jesus, and through their dialogue she recognizes her identity as a Samaritan woman—"a despised heretic and an outcaste half-breed."[40] Dube concludes that such a decolonizing reading of the Samaritan woman's story challenges readers "to acknowledge and embrace their Samaritan social spaces of heretics and half-breeds."[41]

Dube suggests decolonizing the story of the Samaritan woman by rewriting it from a contemporary colonized woman's perspective, with the purpose of conscientizing the colonized to recognize and acknowledge their identities as contemporary Samaritan women. While it is crucial to help the colonized recognize their colonized identities, a postcolonial reading for preaching must move beyond simply the awareness of a colonized identity toward transforming it into a postcolonial identity of the self. Moreover, the Samaritan woman is not the only subject who needs identity transformation in the story; so too does Jesus, who is living in the intergroup conflicts between Jews and Samaritans within the colonies of imperial Rome. Thus, a postcolonial reading for preaching is to reinterpret the story of the Samaritan woman as a story of the formation of a new identity as a postcolonial self.

Taking this story personally, when I focus on the dialogue between the Samaritan woman and Jesus by reflecting on

CHAPTER 1

contemporary Asian American women's experiences, it is a story about postcolonial identity, rather than merely an imperial mission story as Dube understands it. Asian American women live in predominantly white North American society as immigrants and the children of immigrants. They have come from many countries from the Far East to Southwest Asia and the Pacific islands, through different time periods from the late nineteenth century to the present. Willingly or unwillingly, many left homelands that had become poverty-stricken, politically turmoiled, or destroyed by war as a consequence of the colonial imperialism of Western countries or Japan. They wanted to pursue a better future for their own and their children's lives in North America. Although their native languages, historical and sociopolitical backgrounds, and religious and cultural roots are as diverse as all the countries on the continent of Asia and in the Pacific, and although their reasons for immigrating and current living conditions in North America are as varied as their socioeconomic and educational statuses, they, as racial minority people in the white dominant American society, experience in common sociocultural, religious, and generational conflicts and identity confusion.

Along with other racial and ethnic minority people in North America, Asian American women experience systemic racism, tokenism, cultural imperialism, and other forms of discrimination in their workplaces and other sectors of society. They also carry the baggage of the perpetual foreigner syndrome and the model minority stereotype. No matter how many generations of their families have lived in North America as legal citizens, they are often treated as foreigners by being frequently asked, "Where are you from?"; "Where are you really from?"; and "Why don't you go back to your country?" The model minority stereotype is a dangerous myth causing American majority people to ignore the diverse socioeconomic conditions and educational statuses of Asian immigrants struggling to fit into white American society. Above all, sexism is at the core of the Asian American woman's experience. Deeply embedded in both American society and their own ethnic communities, sexism functions as a major force oppressing Asian American women with invisibility and exclusion, and being subjected to enforced silence in decision-making, both at home and in the workplace. Sexism also denigrates their bodies and sexuality as exploitable objects, thereby trivializing them as if they were commodities. These experiences of "dual liminality and marginalization"[42] discourage many Asian American women from living as holistic human beings and equal citizens, perpetuating a sense of powerlessness that extends to self-abasement, despair, hopelessness, and helplessness.[43]

Reflecting on these negative experiences for Asian American women, I imagine the dialogue scene in the story, not in terms of a hierarchical relationship between the inferior Samaritan woman and the superior Jesus, but as one between equal conversational partners. According to the Synoptic Gospels, Jesus faces three temptations in the wilderness just before launching his Messianic ministry, a sort of entrance exam into his three-year program for his Messiahship. However, the Gospel of John doesn't include that story. Instead, Jesus' qualifications to be the Messiah are tested by the Samaritan woman. Yes, he is tested in Samaria, territory of a despised enemy, and by that local woman, a victim of the victims of Roman colonial imperialism. During Jesus' time, Samaritans were suffering extreme forms of economic, political, and religious oppression and exploitation at the hands of the Romans, as well as by the religious and economic power of the Jerusalem temple.[44] The Samaritan woman's three questions are deeply related to her daily lived experiences in this colonial condition, and now she interrogates Jesus to discern if he can be Messiah to herself and her people:

Question Number One: Why do you ask me for water? Don't you know you Jews and we Samaritans should not associate with each other? Why do you break the boundary fortified through the long history of relationship between you Jews and my people, the

Samaritans (v. 9)? Jesus answers, "I want to break that boundary of enmity, from which both your people and my people have drunken the water of prejudice, discrimination, jealousy, and competition that makes them endlessly thirsty. I want them to drink living water from the deep fountain beneath the boundary—'a spring of water gushing up to eternal life' (v.14), and of love to quench their thirst" (vv. 10–15).

Question Number Two: I am a woman who does not meet manmade social norms. Why, then, do you care about me (vv. 16–17)? Jesus answers, "I know you and want to connect you to God's radical love. No matter how people identify you, I remind you that you are a child of God. Nothing can separate you from the love of God" (vv. 18–19).

Question Number Three: Tell me who is right, your people or my people, in worshiping God? Jesus answers, "We Jews have said that 'You worship what you do not know; we worship what we know, for salvation is from the Jews' (v. 22). But the worship that is bound to the rules and policies of the privileged, rather than to spirit and truth, is meaningless (v. 23). Soon we may be allowed to worship in neither your place of worship nor mine by the authority of this world (v. 20). But we don't have to be afraid or discouraged, for God is spirit and is not confined in a physical location. Let us worship God in spirit and truth wherever we are (v. 24)."

The dialogue between Jesus and the Samaritan woman is a process of "mutual recognition" of their identities, for the three questions are about the identity involved in socio-historical, ethical, and religious conditions. Jesus recognizes the Samaritan woman as a member of God's family, and she recognizes who Jesus is by his answers—a boundary-breaker between Jews and Samaritans and between women and men, a boundary-connector between the center and the margins of society, and a boundary-transcender of religions and ideologies. Through this mutual recognition, Jesus passes the entrance exam for his Messiahship.

Jesus as a boundary-breaker, boundary-connector, and boundary-transcender represents the postcolonial self that crosses the ethnic, gender, and religious boundaries that divided people in the imperial Roman world. The postcolonial self is free from exclusive views on humanity and embraces the other beyond their differences. Jesus' identity as a postcolonial self illuminates the potential of the Samaritan woman's identity. Just as smart examinees sometimes challenge their examiners to think differently, so does Jesus in his oral exam, by making the examiner ask herself the question, "Can I live like Jesus as a boundary-breaker, boundary-connector, and boundary-transcender?"

Therefore, preaching Jesus as the Messiah in John's Gospel means preaching him as the model of a postcolonial self and inviting listeners and their churches to this new identity, to live it out in our complex neo- and postcolonial world as postcolonial selves. What kind of homiletical strategies might then be helpful for preaching Jesus as a postcolonial self?

Homiletical Strategies

Reading the story of the Samaritan woman based on Asian American women's experiences is like playing "contrapuntal" music. Unlike traditional music, contrapuntal or polyphonic music is a weaving together of independent melodic lines to produce a beautiful, harmonious whole. Although contrapuntal music has no clear "tonal center," each line has a unique tune and combines with other lines to create harmony. In his book, *Culture and Imperialism*, Said insightfully emphasizes the significance of "the contrapuntal lines of a global analysis" in postcolonial literary and cultural criticism.[45] In his view, "the ecology of literature's new and expanded meaning cannot be attached to only one essence or to the discrete idea of one thing," because it has a multiplicity of perspectives, often implicit and hidden. He compares the multiple meanings of literature to "contrapuntal lines" in music.[46]

Likewise, the image of Jesus as a boundary-breaker, boundary-connector, and boundary-transcender, based on a postcolonial reading of the Samaritan woman's story, can be seen as one of multiple views on the postcolonial self, a unique contrapuntal line.[47] It participates in a harmonious whole with other liberating messages clarifying who Jesus is and what he is doing to make human life human in our neo- and postcolonial world here and now. Preaching this postcolonial image of Jesus is also like playing contrapuntal music. It is a unique contrapuntal line in harmony with preaching other postcolonial images of Jesus.

Creating contrapuntal line preaching of Jesus as a boundary-breaker, boundary-connector, and boundary-transcender is preaching the humanizing work of Jesus. By searching for his presence and activity in our neo- and postcolonial world, we help listeners transform their identities into their postcolonial selves. How then can preaching bring such transformation? Here we can return to my postcolonial reading of the Samaritan woman's story. In the beginning of the story, we find Jesus in Samaria, a unique geopolitical region of the marginalized Roman colonies. Next, his humanizing activity happens in dialogue with a colonized Samaritan woman. Her lived experiences as a Samaritan and a despised woman then provide guiding questions for their conversation and eventually lead both to a recognition of their identities as postcolonial selves.

This reading implies two crucial homiletical strategies for preaching Jesus as a postcolonial self. The first is to listen to the marginalized voices of the colonized in both past and present in their social locations. Whether they are part of our congregations or not, we preachers need to listen to their stories, directly through interviews and other formal and informal conversations, or indirectly by reading their stories and watching movies and documentaries about their lives.

The second homiletical strategy is to use dialogue as an effective homiletical tool for creating a third space, in which listeners are invited to reflect on their identities in a new way. Dialogue is a process of conversation, and in preaching it can be conducted in two ways. One is between the personal and collective stories of colonized people and biblical stories. Dialogue between these stories involves a hermeneutical dimension. As philosopher Stephen Crites explains, stories are "sophisticated activities of consciousness" that recall the images and symbols that "lodged in memory into new configurations, reordering past experience."[48] Dialogue between the stories of the colonized and the characters in the Bible through a postcolonial hermeneutical process has multiple possibilities for identity formation and the potential to create a third space in which listeners engage in a conversation to change and recognize themselves as new beings with new identities.

The other means of dialogue is a sermon crafted in a dialogical style. Traditionally, Christian preaching has taken the form of a monologue following a unilateral direction from top to bottom or from pulpit to pew, by using the three-point-and-a-poem or other kinds of lecture styles, with listeners regarded as passive recipients rather than active participants in the event of preaching. The dialogical style of preaching, however, considers listeners equal conversation partners and expects their participation in preaching from the beginning stage of sermon formation to performance in words or in physical expressions. Such openness requires the preacher's creativity and imagination. For example, the preacher can invite congregants into a Bible study to have a conversation on a particular biblical text that is to be preached on a coming Sunday. A sermon can be scripted as a dialogue, or a multicharacter performance, in which some congregants represent the diverse voices of the colonized, converging in collaboration with biblical voices in the process of meaning-making. And preaching can include congregational songs and liturgical dances as responses during preaching. Such shared preaching with congregants provides listeners with opportunities to participate in creating a third space, where the Spirit of God is present and at work transforming their identities into postcolonial selves, the active agents of God's reconciling work.

These homiletical strategies are just two among many possible creative ideas for preaching Jesus as a postcolonial self. Preachers are invited to further create effective homiletical strategies to help listeners and their communities rethink their identities. Through effective preaching, they are reminded of what they are supposed to be as followers of Jesus in our neo- and postcolonial world and are empowered to participate in God's reconciling work as boundary-breakers, boundary-connectors, and boundary-transcenders.

CHAPTER 2

Preaching Jesus as Postcolonial Song

PREACHING IS A PRACTICAL THEOLOGICAL EXERCISE, A DISCI-pline of Christian theology in which theory and practice relate dialectically to one other in the search for a truthful way of life in various sociocultural and historical contexts. Preaching Jesus through new postcolonial images is a practical theological discipline in the sense that the aim is to help the preacher and listeners discern what God is doing and what God is calling us to do in today's world and to inspire them to participate in God's reconciling work to make our world more human.

Contemporary practical theologians understand their field to be a rational pursuit of "practical wisdom," based on Aristotle's term *phronesis*. According to Aristotle, *phronesis* means "a reasoned and true state of capacity to act with regard to human goods" or "a virtue" that follows "a course of reasoning."[1] As a result, theologians identify practical wisdom as "practical reasoning," which brings about "intelligent human action" in any particular time and place.[2] Or, simply put, the rational discernment of "the right course of action in particular circumstances."[3] However, preaching Jesus from a postcolonial perspective challenges this understanding of practical wisdom, because preaching Jesus with postcolonial images is an imaginative act that involves more than reasoning. This requires of both preachers and listeners the ability to make meaning through a certain mental process of imagining. In discerning such practical wisdom, i.e., what God is doing to make human life more human in our world, a postcolonial imagination is an essential part of practical discernment.

This chapter is concerned with the imagination and its role in preaching Jesus from a postcolonial perspective. The first section explores the nature and function of the postcolonial imagination as a shared channel for the human spirit and the divine Spirit. The second section uses a practical theological method to read the story of Mary's pregnancy and her song in Luke 1:26–56 through a postcolonial imagination, reflecting on Native American people's experiences in North America. The third section presents the new image of Jesus in the form of a postcolonial song based on that reading, while the last section suggests some effective homiletical strategies for preaching Jesus as such a song.

Preaching and the Postcolonial Imagination

The first question when exploring the postcolonial imagination concerns the word "imagination." This word has been defined from multiple perspectives over time and is often used to describe the process behind artistic creativity, fantasy, scientific discovery, and invention. In other words, people tend to understand imagination as the image-making power of the mind, or that which lies behind the act of creating or producing something not previously known. This understanding has been criticized for its connection with nineteenth-century Romantic views of art, and the implication of an opposition to reason. However, philosopher Mark Johnson argues in *The Body in the Mind* that imagination should not be considered separate from reason because it is "our capacity to organize mental representations, especially precepts, images, and image schemata) into meaningful, coherent unities."[4] Another philosopher and theologian, Patrick Sherry, goes further with his comprehensive understanding of imagination. He writes in *Spirit and Beauty* that imagination involves not only the reasoning part of the mind but is also "the whole mind working in a certain way, involving perception, feeling, and reasoning."[5] Thus, imagination is an active power for combining ideas and creating something new by mediating memories and present experiences with future actions, events, and hope. It is one of the most advanced human faculties, involved also in various types of head-, heart-, contemplative, and action-oriented spirituality.[6]

If memories and experiences are essential components of imagination, as Sherry explains, our imaginations are limited because our memories and experiences are partial and fragmented. They are confined to our limited life experiences and imperfect recall. If we seek the wholeness of the truth, we must stretch our imaginations by sharing the memories and experiences of others. Otherwise, our imaginings might become egotistic and even harmful to others. It is noteworthy that in her essay, "Ungrounded Innocence," European American feminist scholar Karen Bray pairs such an unhealthy imagination with the colonial imagination. She criticizes the colonial imagination in Christian theology and practice as corrupted, saying that American Protestant Christianity, founded on the ground of European American Puritan culture, has legitimized white supremacy as "divinely ordained" and whiteness as a "cherished property."[7] She traces how this colonial imagination has evolved into a "myth" through Christian preaching, liturgy, and ritual, and urges that it be decolonized through "the active dismantling of structures that have sheltered all white Christians for far too long."[8]

The colonial imagination is "a diseased social imagination," to use theologian Willie Jennings's term.[9] Our individual and social imaginations also remain partial and biased and may result in an illusion divorced from reality in the larger world. At worst, they may be "diseased" by selfish ideologies, such as racism, sexism, ableism, homophobia, and white supremacy. Yet, when we stretch our imaginations by sharing the memories and experiences of those who live in different social locations, it is possible for us to come closer to the wholeness of the truth. The postcolonial imagination is stretched by sharing memories and experiences, especially with the colonized of both past and present, so that we might envision a new world for all the creatures of God. At this point, the postcolonial imagination becomes a shared social imagination, pointing the way for people to envision their social existence together with others.

The postcolonial imagination can be expanded upon in three ways. First, it is fundamentally shared between the colonized and the colonizers, and can be used to imagine our world collaboratively in a fresh, new way. Postcolonial feminist theologian Kwok Pui-lan explains the postcolonial imagination as a shared imagination with three distinct yet interwoven modes—historical, dialogical, and diasporic.[10] The historical imagination is born out of the experiences of the enslaved and colonized of the past, including biblical times, as well as the present. She insists that their voices and their unattended stories in the history of Western colonialization be retrieved as part of the process of imagining a new world.[11] By dialogical imagination, Kwok means a deliberate strategy for reading biblical texts in dialogue with non-Western myths, stories, and religious resources thereby creating a deepened engagement with postcolonial theories and cultural studies.[12] She argues that there is no real or historical Jesus in the sense of a pristine Christian origin. Instead, the notion of "Jesus/Christ" has been a hybridized concept from the beginning.[13] Through dialogical imagination, she presents new images of Jesus Christ, such as Jesus the Black Christ, Jesus the Corn Mother, Jesus the Feminine Shakti, and Jesus as Bi/Christ.[14] When Kwok discusses the diasporic imagination, she understands "diaspora" in general terms, to include all those who have migrated from formerly colonized countries to the metropolitan West for various reasons and in many situations. She explains that a diasporic imagination based on such diverse lived experiences helps us see our world through others' eyes, and hence decenter the cultural norms of Eurocentric Christianity.[15]

Preaching through these three modes of the postcolonial imagination presents a stark contrast to the postliberal way of preaching. Drawing on Hans Frei and George Lindbeck's cultural-linguistic approach and intratextuality, postliberal homiletician Charles Campbell argues that Jesus of Nazareth is not "merely a symbol of a myth,"[16] because myths are stories "echoing universal experience." Instead, he emphasizes that the story of Jesus is rendered through "the ascriptive logic of the gospels," which speak of "the identity of a particular person whose life, death, and resurrection accomplish God's purposes for the world."[17] Campbell states that this unique story of Jesus is the core of the Christian canon and has been interpreted through "the church's tradition of literal reading."[18] Thus, the task of preaching, for Campbell, is not to create new images of Jesus Christ, but to teach or witness to Jesus by retelling the church's story of Jesus Christ again and again.[19] For this purpose, Campbell suggests that "expository preaching"[20] and "the form of colonial Puritan sermons,"[21] which use the twofold method of exposition and application, are effective tools for preaching Jesus.

While the postliberal view reminds us of the Bible's significant function as the canon of the Christian community, it idealizes the church by overstating the untranslatability of the story of Jesus. It fails to critically examine its own Eurocentric traditions of biblical interpretation and colonial proclamation about Jesus Christ. Moreover, as theologian Kathryn Tanner critically points out in *Theories of Culture*, postliberal theology understands Christian identity as "self-contained and self-originating," despite the cultural mix in the actual practices of a Christian way of life.[22] As a result, just as Lindbeck and Frei's postliberal theology is "a totalitarian modern approach that overlooks the fluidity of culture" and that "fosters a narrowly constructed and tightly bound view of religious identity,"[23] so too Campbell's postliberal homiletics fails to consider the complexity of cultural hybridity in Christian identity. Furthermore, it ignores the significance of preaching Jesus through new images in our neo- and postcolonial world.

The second characteristic of the postcolonial imagination is that it is acquired not only through a critical academic discipline such as Kwok describes with her three modes of postcolonial imagination, but also through a spiritual discipline that leads us to encounter the presence of God in everyday life. The postcolonial imagination exists for the discernment of Christian practical wisdom, and imagination is an attribute of God that functions as a spiritual channel connecting the divine Spirit with the human spirit. Like the Möbius strip where the two ends of the paper are attached with a half-twist and become one surface, the divine Spirit is infused into the human spirit to become one through imagination.[24] This relationality between human and divine can be formed through the daily spiritual practices of prayer and actions connected to achieving loving communion with God and others.[25]

Postcolonial imagination is evoked through this spiritual practice. It is the conduit through which the preacher discerns Christian practical wisdom in accommodation with the Spirit. The Holy Spirit vitalizes and liberates the preacher's spirit, which is inspired to create something new: new images and new patterns of meaning that are different from those of the colonial imagination. Through a postcolonial imagination, preachers can listen to the voice of the Spirit and discern the presence and activity of God among the others who are colonized and marginalized in our society and be stimulated to preach what God calls us all to be. The postcolonial imagination, therefore, is a divine gift, "the God-power in the soul."[26] It is inspired by faith, which it in turn strengthens.[27]

The third characteristic of the postcolonial imagination is that it is a medium to connect the preacher and listeners with those of diverse experiences across racial, ethnic, gender, and class lines in our complex, globalized world. By listening attentively to the lived experiences of the marginalized and colonized, both past and present, and by sharing their visions for a better world, the preacher can inspire listeners to see things from an unfamiliar point of view and discover empathy and solidarity toward those other people. At this point, a postcolonial imagination is, as theologian and civil rights leader Howard Thurman describes it, "the *angelos* [messenger] of God" who makes possible a "great adventure in human relations" across racial and ethnic groups.[28]

How then does the postcolonial imagination make a difference in preaching Jesus? Preaching Jesus through a postcolonial imagination is a visionary and creative act for the purpose of meaning-making appropriate to our neo- and postcolonial contexts. It is a way of responding to existential, theological, and ethical questions such as: What does it mean to be human? Where is God and what is God doing to make and keep human life human? What kind of a world do we want to bequeath to the next generations? And what, as members of the body of Christ, are we to do for the new vision? Preachers can probe these questions and create new images, metaphors, and symbols of Jesus through a postcolonial imagination, and thereby help their listeners reconsider their personal and communal identities reflexively. For example, the postcolonial image of Jesus presented in the previous chapter functions as a metaphor. While it is rooted in a particular historical and sociocultural context, the identity of Jesus as a postcolonial self is not confined to a reaction against solely the first-century colonial culture of the Roman Empire. Instead, the identity of Jesus is open-ended and fluid, pregnant with potential for more relevant images that can respond to those existential, theological, and ethical questions that arise in today's neo- and postcolonial context.

The postcolonial imagination therefore makes it possible for preachers to open a new range of thoughts and feelings about Jesus. Unlike the colonial imagination, the postcolonial imagination rejects a European Christology that depicts Jesus as a symbol of Western superiority or the ideal of a morally perfect individual. Instead, it allows preachers to create a third space. As explained in the first chapter, a third space signifies "productive capacities" through which "the existing exclusive colonial status quo is subverted and new signs of identity are initiated.[29] In a third space, the Holy Spirit accommodates the human spirit so that the preacher and listeners might reconfigure their Christian identity through a new image of Jesus, a symbol of one who affirms life, dignity, and freedom in our neo- and postcolonial world.

A Reading through the Postcolonial Imagination

In addition to the new image of Jesus as a postcolonial self, another contrapuntal line of preaching Jesus is to preach Jesus as a postcolonial song. This image comes from reading Luke's account of Mary's pregnancy through a postcolonial imagination. In Luke, the story of Mary's pregnancy immediately follows Elizabeth's praise of God for her own miraculous pregnancy in 1:25, where she proclaims: "The Lord . . . has shown his favor and taken away my disgrace among the people." Mary's story is then made up of three vignettes with a concluding remark: In verses 26 to 38, the angel Gabriel appears to Mary and announces that she will be pregnant through the intervention of the Holy Spirit. From verses 39 to 45, Mary visits Elizabeth and is convinced that her pregnancy indicates God's favor. From verses 46 to 55, Mary responds to God by singing a song, "The Magnificat." Finally, verse 57 concludes the story by saying that Mary stays with Elizabeth for about three months.

Generally, this story is regarded as an Advent text.[30] However, the Christian calendar includes the "Feast of the Annunciation" on March 25, a day during Lent or the Easter season, and the story of Mary's pregnancy is read as the main text for that day. It is also noteworthy that in *A Women's Lectionary for the Whole Church*, Wilda Gafney includes the story on the day of the "Feast of the

Ever-Blessed Virgin Mary" after Pentecost.[31] Hence, this story is applied to the various Christological themes of Lent, Easter, and Pentecost, as well as those of Advent, and provides the theological origin of God's grace in and through Jesus Christ.

Reading this story with a postcolonial imagination requires a dual vision from the preacher: one for the world in the text and one for the world in a context for preaching. For such a reading strategy, Richard Osmer's four tasks of interpretation are helpful. In his book, *Practical Theology*, Osmer identifies the first task as descriptive and empirical, focusing on the question, "What is going on?" The second task is the scientific exploration of the question, "Why is this going on?" The third task is the normative interpretation or discernment of "what *ought* to be going on?" And the last task is the pragmatic answer to the question, "How might we respond?"[32] While Osmer suggests this fourfold interpretive task as the process of "practical reasoning" to discern practical wisdom, it is also a useful hermeneutical process for reading the biblical story through a postcolonial imagination for preaching.

The traditional reading of the story focuses on Mary as the main character, with Elizabeth in a supporting role. Yet, when we read the story through a postcolonial imagination, they are equally important, for their experiences illustrate the condition of women in a patriarchal colonial culture. These two women are cousin-sisters with a wide age gap, as much as a generation apart. Yet their strenuous search to understand their unusual pregnancies leads them to sisterhood in the Spirit, which is eventually developed into discipleship. And in his Gospel, Luke presents their sisterhood as the overture to the good news of Jesus Christ.

What is going on with these two women in the story, then, and why is it going on? While Osmer emphasizes the significance of quantitative and qualitative research for understanding what is going on, and scientific studies for exploring why this is going on, an empathetic approach is also important when reading the story through a postcolonial imagination. In first-century Jewish patriarchal society, women were valued for their reproductive ability, and especially for giving birth to sons. Many women around the globe today are still suffering in such patriarchal cultures, where they are treated as instruments of reproduction. I can imagine how excited Elizabeth, probably already in her menopausal years, was about her miraculous pregnancy, as Luke describes her reaction as one of amazement and joy. However, I can also imagine how difficult and complicated pregnancy might have been in later life by recalling my own experience of childbirth. Yet Luke is silent about that. As a male, he may have been ignorant of women's experiences with pregnancy or didn't consider them important.

Mary's pregnancy story is very different from Elizabeth's. According to Luke, Mary is a virgin, betrothed to Joseph, and living in Nazareth, a small, impoverished peasant village in Galilee. Then God sends the angel Gabriel to tell her that the Holy Spirit will be over her and she will bear a child, the Son of the Most High. In traditional Christian theology, this announcement is the very core of the doctrine of the incarnation and a source of belief in the divinity of Jesus Christ.

However, a historical imagination leads us to suspect Luke's romantic description of Mary's pregnancy. For example, in her book, *The Illegitimacy of Jesus*, feminist biblical theologian Jane Schaberg imagines the possibility that Mary might have been raped, either by a countryman or by a Roman soldier.[33] In other words, this young teenage girl might have been a victim of sexual violence. Although this claim is debatable, there is no doubt that such an interpretation is plausible, considering the historical, sociocultural, and political context of the story. It is possible Mary was a double victim—a victim of the violence of Roman colonial imperialism and of the patriarchal Jewish social and legal system. According to historical records around the time when Jesus was born, Roman soldiers invaded Galilee and destroyed the town of Nazareth, killing and raping women.[34] We know that sexual violence in colonial patriarchal society is common even in our contemporary world. The Gospel of Matthew also records that Mary's pregnancy out of wedlock placed her in danger of being stoned to death under the Jewish law of adultery. It is for this reason that Joseph, her fiancé, wanted to divorce her quietly to protect her from disgrace and life-threatening danger (Matt. 1:18–25; Deut. 22:20–24).

The traditional image of Mary is that of an obedient, naïve, and passive woman who accepts her mysterious pregnancy without any decision-making of her own. Alternatively, she is understood as a surrogate mother whose feminine body was borrowed so that God might bear God's Son. However, when we read Luke's story through a postcolonial imagination channeling the human spirit and the divine Spirit, we find that God is working to humanize Mary's life in the colonial patriarchal world. While Mary is mute in Matthew's account, Luke gives her a voice by telling her pregnancy story, not as the story of a victim, but as a story of God's mercy. According to Luke, God is directly involved in Mary's life, transforming her identity from a victim of the patriarchal and colonial violence into God's agent. God sends the angel Gabriel and her cousin-sister Elizabeth at this critical moment in Mary's life to convince her that God is working through her pregnancy. It is the story of God's grace for subservient women in a first-century Roman colony. It is also one with the potential to be interpreted as the story of God's grace for those who are victims of twenty-first century forms of colonialism.

Luke also indicates that Elizabeth is a spiritual being, living in and with the Holy Spirit. She is able to see what God is doing to make human life human, not only in her life, but also in the lives of others. She quickly recognizes Mary as God does, and understands God's grand plan when Mary runs into her house in fear and perplexity. With her own embodied joy leaping in her womb, Elizabeth prophesies God's promise to Mary and her baby in a loud voice. Indeed, Elizabeth is fully human, a spiritual being, partnering with God in seeing the world as the Spirit moves.

When Mary encounters Elizabeth, the Holy Spirit in Elizabeth moves into Mary's body and soul, and she stands in a Third Space, a creative holy ground, and imagines a new world, a world in which her powerless colonized people—the lowly and poor—receive God's mercy. Mary sings "what ought to be going on" for her people. In her song, she first praises God's mercy on her and then proclaims God's victorious deeds for her oppressed fellows:

> Your mercy is on those who fear you,
> from generation to generation.
> You have shown strength with your arm.
> You have scattered the proud in their hearts' conceit.
> You have put down the mighty from their thrones,
> and have lifted up the lowly.
> You have filled the hungry with good things,
> and have sent the rich away empty.[35]

Roman Catholic feminist theologian Elizabeth Johnson declares that this is a revolutionary song of salvation in a concrete social, economic, and political context. People are hungry because of triple taxes exacted for Rome, the local government, and the temple. The lowly are crushed because of the mighty on their thrones in Rome and their deputies in the provinces. Now, with the nearness of the messianic age, a new social order of justice is at hand, and Mary's song praises God for a salvation that involves concrete transformation.[36]

Mary, a poor, first-century Galilean peasant woman living in an occupied territory of the Roman Empire, struggling for survival and dignity, now sings this revolutionary song in the name of God. Although the traditional image of Mary, constructed through a colonial imagination, is of someone obedient, gentle, and sentimentally dreamy, the postcolonial imagination no longer pictures her as a voiceless passive victim of the patriarchal colonial power. Instead, she is a courageous singer, poet, and prophetic preacher, dreaming a new world for herself and her children yet to be born. Her notion of what ought to be going on is "radical economic reversal" and a "radical alternative to the rule of Rome." It is a radical imagination quite unlike the colonial imagination that is grounded in "the insatiable greed of the powerful at the expense of the vulnerable."[37]

Native American scholar Tink Tinker characterizes the colonial imagination with the term, "thingification." He explains:

> The colonizer saw human beings in the territories they colonized as mere objects or things to be used—Africans, Caribbean folk, American Indians, and the like. And this colonizers' thingifying imaginary was never limited to human beings alone but extends to seeing the whole world as mere things or objects to be dominated by themselves (and owned) for the enrichment, enjoyment and comfort of themselves.[38]

Another North American indigenous scholar, Kyle Whyte, also reminds us that economic disparity and the destruction of the ecosystem are inevitably connected as a consequence of the colonial imagination:

> The massive environmental changes imposed on Indigenous peoples by U.S. and Canadian colonization and settlement include deforestation, draining wetlands, damming, recreation, mining, commercial agriculture, shipping, petrochemical and industrial manufacturing, and burning fossil fuels. . . . Settlement affects ecosystems, including hydrological systems and wetlands that support wild rice, that are crucial to Anishinaabe peoples for exercising moral relationships.[39]

Moreover, Native American feminist scholar Leanne Simpson indicates that "the destruction of land through resource extraction, environmental contamination, imposed poverty, heteropatriarchy, or colonial gendered violence"[40] is also the product of the colonial imagination.

These Native American voices make us aware that economic justice is deeply connected with cultural and environmental justice, and this worldview and value system lead us to interpret Mary's song as an alternative imagination, that is, as a postcolonial eschatological imagination that envisions a new world for all of creation—human and nonhuman creatures alike who have "been groaning in labor pains until now" (Rom. 8:22). Thus, Mary's song is a postcolonial song for life, not just human life, but the life of all living creatures, with "respect for the land, water, and air."[41] It is not merely about stewardship, but is about "partnership with other creatures of earth; and a way of living and working that achieves a balance between use and replenishment of all resources."[42] At this point, Mary's postcolonial song is a visionary eschatological imagination. Mary's lyrics reclaim and promote economic, cultural, environmental, and social justice for the sake of the well-being of all creation. By singing this song, she uproots the colonial imagination and plants instead a postcolonial imagination.

Jesus as Postcolonial Song

Where is Jesus in Luke's narrative? He is unborn. Yet the unborn Jesus is the source of Mary's eschatological postcolonial imagination. In other words, the unborn Jesus is a proleptical sign of God's humanizing activity. Luke ascribes Mary's song to Jesus, and Mary's song is a preview of his future identity. Jesus must have listened to Mary's song from the day of conception through the developmental stages in her womb. Even after he was born, he would have grown up listening to his mother's prophetic revolutionary song again and again. Indeed, he was a preacher's kid!

Later, Jesus' ministry became a movement of spreading his mother's song that it might come true on the earth.

It is thus no wonder that Luke inserts the Isaiah text into Jesus' inaugural address in 4:18–19,[43] "the Spirit of the Lord is on me, because he has anointed me to proclaim good news to the poor."[44] Biblical commentators and feminist theologians understand Mary's song in light of the long tradition of female Jewish singers, from Miriam with her tambourine (Exod. 15:2–21) to Deborah (Judg. 5:1–31), Hannah (1 Sam. 2:1–10), and Judith (Jdt. 16:1–17), who all sang victory songs of the oppressed.[45] Yet Mary's song is also a preamble to Jesus' ministry, alluding to his identity in line with the ancient prophets, continuing through his mother Mary to our own contemporary visionaries. The unborn Jesus in the story therefore functions as a sign of the coming reign of God. As Miroslav Volf states in *The End of Memory*, "a new vision for a better world arises from the realm of what is not yet, from outside, from God's promise."[46] In this sense, Jesus is a postcolonial song, the vision of our hearts. He is the sign of God's grace symbolizing that God's future has already come here and now to make human life more human in our colonial, neocolonial, and postcolonial world. Through Jesus in Mary's womb, we can imagine our world differently and act differently.

How then might we respond to the sign of the coming reign of God? By recognizing the identity of Jesus as a postcolonial song, we recognize our own identity reflexively in a new way and respond to God's grace by preaching Jesus as our contemporary freedom song. Simpson defines freedom from a Native American perspective as follows: First, it is a state of "the absence of coercion, hierarchy, or authoritarian power" of colonialism. Second, freedom means "connectivity based on the sanctity of the land." Third, freedom is the right to practice "the love we have for our families, our language, our way of life," and last, freedom includes "relationships based on deep reciprocity, respect, noninterference, [and] self-determination."[47] Simpson also suggests that to achieve this freedom, the colonizers must stop "plundering the land and the climate and using Indigenous peoples' bodies to fuel their economy," and "find a way of living in the world that is not based on violence and exploitation."[48] For we need to live a different present if we want to create a different future, and if we want to live in a different present, we have to allow it to change us.[49]

If our listeners are middle- and upper-middle-class American citizens benefiting from the privileges of American colonial imperialism and are satisfied with the ways things are, they may struggle with the message of this postcolonial song. In fact, Mary's revolutionary song is a dangerous memory. In the British colonial era of the nineteenth century, the authorities banned the recitation of this freedom song in Indian Anglican churches. Fast-forwarding, in the mid-1970s this song was banned in Argentina after the "Mothers of the Disappeared" used it to call for protests against the ruling military junta. During the 1980s, the military government of Guatemala also banned public recitation of Mary's song.[50] Despite such a danger, the reason why we should preach Jesus as postcolonial song is because we know we cannot bequeath our world as it is to our children and our children's children. We need homiletical ideas and strategies to make our preaching appeal to diverse people.

HOMILETICAL STRATEGIES

Preaching Jesus as a postcolonial song does not merely condemn Western colonialism and deconstruct the colonial imagination. Additionally, its goal is to create a third space, in which solidarity is built through a reciprocal recognition that goes beyond the boundaries of race, ethnicity, gender, and class. As Simpson elaborates, reciprocal recognition is a process of self-reflexivity through which we see another being's light, and then reflect that light back to ourselves, thereby fully comprehending that other being with all our thoughts and feelings.[51] Through reciprocal recognition, "deep solidarity"[52] with those who live in different life situations from our own is possible. As theologian Joerg Rieger puts it, deep solidarity is rooted in the critical analysis of unjust conditions in our neo- and postcolonial world in its various forms, and is something that forces us to strive for the common good of humanity with "the power of resistance."[53]

One homiletical strategy for building solidarity through reciprocal recognition is dialectical communication. The movement of such communication goes from thesis through antithesis to synthesis. It invites listeners to understand the biblical story from a postcolonial perspective (the thesis), to critically reflect on their identity as constructed by colonial imagination in order to renew it (the antithesis), and then to renew their identity through participation in deep solidarity (the synthesis).[54] A sermon following such a dialectical movement is not interested in moralistic teaching about love and charity. The ultimate concern is to transform listeners' colonial imaginations into postcolonial ones and help them act these out through participation in the work of human liberation and solidarity.

There are many patterns of preaching, such as the traditional three-point-and-poem style, verse-by-verse expository preaching, and the narrative preaching of the New Homiletic. While these various forms can be used creatively in designing the dialectical movement in a sermon, some literary genres less familiar to preachers can be useful also. For example, if you are an Episcopalian or Roman Catholic preacher, your seven-minute homily can be crafted as a song. You can update Mary's song into a contemporary freedom song by reflecting on the experiences of those living on the margins of society as the colonized, and by standing in solidarity with them.

Writing a community letter is another possible literary method for preaching Jesus as a postcolonial song. This past summer I had the opportunity to preach a sermon from the story of Mary's pregnancy to a mostly middle- and upper-middle-class European American Christian congregation. To scatter their colonial imagination and instead plant a postcolonial imagination in their hearts, I wrote a letter to Mary and Elizabeth on their behalf, and in it I followed a dialectical movement.[55] The letter began:

> Dear Mary and Elizabeth,
> Greetings from the United States,
> from a group of church leaders on the other side of the planet,
> two-thousand years after you.

The first movement, the thesis, understands the story by standing in Elizabeth and Mary's shoes in a first-century Judean colony of the Roman Empire, and praising their sisterhood in the Spirit and Mary's courage to sing a revolutionary song. The second movement, the antithesis, critically reflects on ourselves as privileged American citizens and negates Mary's song, by saying,

> We are like a new Roman Empire, living like Romans.
> Slavery, exploitation, and the appropriation of resources from Africa, Asia, and Latin America.
> That is the backbone of our nation's wealth, the benefit of colonialism. . . .
> We are in no great position to sing your song with joy.
> We dare not praise the God who favors your own—
> the colonized, the poor, and the lowly.

The last movement, the synthesis, finds a common concern between the biblical characters and ourselves, which is to seek to bequeath a better world to our children. In this movement we ask Mary and Elizabeth to transmit the Holy Spirit to us so that we may also imagine a new world, and in so doing, sing Jesus as a postcolonial song. The sermon concludes:

Sister Mary and Sister Elizabeth,
Bless us with imagination to live as faithful disciples
of God
in our time of crisis,
as fearlessly and compassionately as you.

As this sermon in the form of a letter illustrates, preaching Jesus as a postcolonial song is a prayer, a communal prayer to the Holy Spirit to help us sing a revolutionary visionary song wholeheartedly, not only in words and melody, but in action. Just as Mary sings a vision for a new world on behalf of her children, so do we, with faith that the Holy Spirit is moving ceaselessly to make a difference in God's creation. By preaching Jesus as a postcolonial song, we share divine pathos and imagination with the world and become "friend[s] of God" and "prophet[s] of the coming age,"[56] just like Mary and Elizabeth.

CHAPTER 3

Preaching Jesus as Postcolonial Child

WHEN WE CRITICALLY REFLECT ON THE HISTORY OF PREACHING in Europe and the United States from a postcolonial perspective, we find that the Western churches have often overlooked the fact that Jesus was a colonized Jew of the Roman Empire with a culturally hybrid identity. Homiletical resources for preaching Jesus, written with Western audiences in mind, largely fail to indicate the impact of this colonized reality on Jesus' identity and ministry. What would it be like if we were to locate the story of Jesus in the cultural context of the Roman Empire and preach him from a postcolonial perspective? This chapter will read the story of Jesus' birth in Matthew from that period perspective and present his identity as a postcolonial child. Among the Nativity stories in the Gospels, Matthew's account of Jesus' escape to Egypt (1:13–26) depicts him as a political refugee. It is a story that challenges us to search for a postcolonial approach to preaching Jesus, given that global migration has become one of the most critical issues of today's world.

The current unprecedented surge in global migration is a direct consequence of hundreds of years of Western colonialism and neocolonialism. Although migration is not new in human history, numbers of migrants traveling from the formerly colonized countries in the global South to the metropoles have drastically increased since the last quarter of the twentieth century. According to the UN High Commissioner for Refugees (UNHCR), in the first months of 2022 alone, 100 million people were forcibly displaced worldwide. Among them, 26.6 million were refugees and 4.4 million asylum-seekers.[1] In addition, at least 12 million Ukrainians left their homes since Russia invaded their country in February 2022.[2] All migrants throughout the world in these times have been likewise involuntarily pushed from their homelands by military, political, and economic forces beyond their control, and are struggling to survive while enduring extraordinary hardships and traumas.

Global migration is a complex and serious phenomenon that intersects with other postcolonial issues, such as racism, sexism, economic injustice, and ecological crises. However, in mass media coverage of these issues and in public discourse, the root causes of these issues are often ignored, and the focus limited to the symptomatic problems. Immigrants, refugees, and asylum-seekers are seen as troublemakers requiring assistance, despite the fact that the majority of them, especially the countless undocumented migrants at the US-Mexico border, are victims of the Western colonial and neocolonial imperialism that extracted the natural and human resources from their countries of origin.

This chapter reflects on the postcolonial issue of migration when proclaiming the good news of God's incarnation in Jesus. The first section evaluates the images of Jesus from a postcolonial perspective, which the Christian church preaches during the Christmas season. The second is a reading of Matthew's account of Jesus' escape to Egypt from a postcolonial feminist point of view. The third presents Jesus as a postcolonial child, a model for all children living similarly in that time, and the last concludes with some homiletical insights and strategies for preaching Jesus as a postcolonial child.

Preaching Jesus as Postcolonial Child

Migration and the Christmas Message

As we know, the Bible contains many passages about immigrants, foreigners, and refugees. Rabbi Jonathan Sack reminds us that, while we might think "You shall love your neighbor as yourself" is the greatest command in the Bible, it is only found in one place: Leviticus 19:18. Yet in more than thirty places, the Bible commands us to love the stranger.[3] Even in Leviticus 19, the command to love our neighbors is followed by the command to love the foreigner (Lev. 19:33–34). Moreover, the greatest migrant story in Christian Scripture concerns the incarnation of God in Jesus Christ becoming a political refugee (Matt. 2:13–23). Despite this, modern theologians and preachers have considered the story of Jesus' escape to Egypt historically unreliable and have often dismissed it from their discourse. For example, in his book, *Preaching Jesus Christ: An Exercise in Homiletic Theology*,[4] David Buttrick does not consider the incarnation and the Nativity stories suitable for preaching and erases them from his Christological themes. Yet those stories have historical and cultural settings, narrative plots, and literary intentions that indicate the identity of the historical Jesus. The story of Jesus' escape to Egypt is a theologically profound source for preaching who God is and what God is doing to make human life human in our neo- and postcolonial world.

This story is included in the *Revised Common Lectionary* for the first Sunday after Christmas in Year A. The congregations of the churches that follow the lectionary will hear this story once every three years. Unlike the stories of the magi and the shepherds, it is neither cozy nor nostalgic, but a fearful and dangerous story with the horrific scene of the massacre of the innocent children in the background. As a result, the Commission for the *Revised Common Lectionary*, made up of white American male scholars, sought to shift the focus of the story away from Jesus' identity as a political refugee, by choosing three other texts for that Sunday that emphasize his divine Lordship instead: Isaiah

63:7–9, Psalm 148, and Hebrews 2:10–18. Biblical commentaries published before the twenty-first century also focused on Jesus' divine Lordship or Sonship being protected by God in discussions of this passage.[5]

Furthermore, as liturgical scholars Michael Jagessar and Stephen Burns remind us, the annual "Festival of Lessons and Carols" from King's College, Cambridge in England does not include the story of Jesus' escape to Egypt. Instead, the Service of Nine Lessons and Carols that was developed in 1880, during "the prime and high noon of the colonial expansion" of England, highlights the magi and shepherd stories. The image of God in those stories is "one who endorses travel to distant places, bringing light to darkened peoples (Isaiah 9:2–7)," which aligns with the colonial imagination that Jagessar and Burns refer to as "White European superiority."[6]

Yet it is worth noting that the fifth-century Latin church instituted the Feast of the Holy Innocents on December 28, highlighting the story of Jesus' escape to Egypt. It was "a grim reminder that there was and is a political cost to the incarnation."[7] Still, most European American Protestant churches do not know about that feast; even if they are aware, they have routinely ignored the event. Consequently, the image of Jesus as a political refugee is rarely proclaimed in the Christian churches. When I taught the course "Prophetic Ministry: Immigration, Refugees, and Displacement," I asked students if they had ever preached or heard a sermon about Jesus as a political refugee. All the white students unanimously replied, "Never!" They also indicated a reluctance to preach Jesus in terms of that image because it wouldn't sound like good news to their listeners—it would introduce an unwelcome note into the season of "merry" Christmas.

But does the story in fact convey good news? And if so, what good news? Reading the story from a postcolonial feminist perspective offers insight into what good news it does contain.

A Postcolonial Feminist Reading

The story of Jesus' escape to Egypt has three parts: First, Joseph takes Mary and Jesus and leaves for Egypt after an angel appears to him in a dream and instructs him to do so (2:13–15). Second, King Herod slaughters all the boys in and around Bethlehem in order to kill Jesus (2:16–18). Third, after an angel informs him that Herod has died (2:19–23), Joseph returns his family back to Israel where they live in the town of Nazareth in Galilee.

To read this story from a postcolonial feminist perspective involves not merely "how" to read it, but "what" to read.[8] Such an approach prioritizes "the unheard or left-out voices"[9] of the colonized, especially the women who are victims of other victims. The male biblical authors of the patriarchal imperial world hid the women's voices, or reduced them to passing references, either wittingly or not. Like a magnifying glass, a postcolonial feminist lens allows us to recognize the invisible or unattended colonized women in the biblical stories by zooming in on them. Such a lens allows us to reappropriate the stories, by drawing out, extending, and giving voice to the women in them through a postcolonial imagination.

The story of Jesus' escape to Egypt is also the story of colonized women—Mary the mother of Jesus, plus the mothers of the infants killed by Herod, himself a vassal king of the Roman empire. Yet, in the story Mary is voiceless, as are the voices of those mothers whose children are victims of horrific imperial violence. Their voices are simply echoed in a passing reference to "Rachel's cry" in Jeremiah 31:15. However, although these women are on the margins of the story, a postcolonial feminist lens brings them to center stage and helps us see them more clearly.

How then might we retrieve their voices to create new meaning from the story? Here again, a postcolonial imagination plays a significant role. One of the functions of this imagination is to the analogical bridge two different worlds—the first-century *Pax Romana* and a twenty-first-century *Pax Americana*—by moving to-and-fro between them. In the analogical process, interdisciplinary studies of the historical, sociocultural, and economic conditions of the two empires are essential for identifying similarities and differences. New Testament scholar Warren Carter informs us that the oppressive imperial power of *Pax Romana* was supported by an imperial ideology that Rome was destined by the gods to rule over other countries. This religious ideology legitimized the oppressive colonial power through socioeconomic, political, military, cultural, and legal means, and benefitted the colonizers at the center and upper levels of the society at the expense of the colonized who dwelt on the periphery and at lower levels.[10]

The stories of Jesus and his family's escape to Egypt and of the massacre of the innocent children illustrate the cruelty of *Pax Romana* in preserving its power and the suffering and pain of the innocent people who were colonized. Even religious leaders, who were supposed to raise a prophetic voice against oppression, complied with it for the sake of their vested interests. As another New Testament scholar, Ched Myers, correctly states, this story is not a fantasy but "an archetypal portrait"[11] of the general circumstance of the Roman colonies both before and after Jesus' birth. While Matthew embellishes the historical data of the infamous violence of Herod the Great in the story, the traumatic experiences of Mary and the other women in this setting could have happened at any time and in any colony of the Roman Empire.[12]

Human history is riddled with colonial imperialism. *Pax Americana* provides an example from the modern West. In his essay, "The Task Ahead," Presbyterian preacher and peace activist William Sloane Coffin asserts that, just as the Roman Empire legitimized its territorial expansion with religious ideology, so too the United States justified its Anglo territorial expansion throughout the last century with the religious ideological concept of "Manifest Destiny." As Charles Evans Hughes, the Secretary of State from 1921 to 1925, dispatched the Marines into Nicaragua for the fourteenth time in that country's history, he announced that America was seeking to establish *Pax Americana*. Thereafter, the US government invaded at least twenty-one countries in Latin American, including Guatemala in 1954, Cuba in 1960, the Dominican Republic in 1965, Chile in 1973, and subsequently El Salvador and Honduras. Moreover, the US government participated in at least twenty-six CIA-led operations throughout the Caribbean basin to institute regime change.[13] *Pax Americana* has benefitted North Americans, just as *Pax Romana* did for the Romans. Now the flow of migrants across the US-Mexico border, from El Salvador, Honduras, Guatemala, Haiti, and other Latin American countries, is one of the tragic consequences of *Pax Americana*.

In the poem "Only Say the Word,"[14] which poet Demetria Martinez writes as a conversation among three women—a Guatemalan Indian, a North American schoolteacher, and a Chimayó native[15]—the Guatemalan Indian woman shares the violent postcolonial condition of her life like this:

> Wood, wood and ash:
> These are the colors of the people
> In Cordero [my village].
> We are dark but lovely,
> Strong, though now broken.
> We live in shadows of guns and jeeps,
> One by one we are disappeared.
> Guards in green uniforms,
> Like statues come to life, terrify.
> After Mass on Sunday
> They tore our saints out of niches,
> Smashed out chalices,
> Threw lots for altar cloths
> Our grandmothers wove.
> My husband learned to read the Bible,
> He memorized the book of Luke.

After a day in the coffee plantations
Neighbors would gather to pray,
To hear my husband read:
"Bienaventurados los pobres,"
Blessed are the poor,
The Kingdom will be ours.
Then, ten men,
No older than seventeen,
The gleam of the devil
In their yellow eyes,
They beat my husband with rifles
Until his face
Was a bloody moon.
I fell on top of him,
I thought he was dead.
Neighbors' cries, like those of dogs
Tortured for fun, rose to heaven,
No guardian angels landed.
My husband lives, but cannot smell
The steam of tortillas and black beans,
Nor the scent of the body
Which bore his four children.
He calls me his "rose,"
But what is a rose without scent?
A paper flower, flat,
Which no one will buy.
Fear, like a fruit pit,
Is lodged in my husband's throat.
He chokes in his sleep, weeps,
Speaks about escaping to the north.[16]

Like Jesus and his family, tens of thousands of children and their families have fled violence, death, and poverty in their home countries in Central and South America, a situation aggravated by the COVID-19 pandemic. Just as Mary and Joseph had to flee to save their son, so too have these families left their countries to save their own and their children's lives. Their hope for their children is, "less suffering and a better life," as the Mexican American theologian Virgilio Elizondo puts it in his book, *The Galilean Journey*.[17] This may be the same hope Mary had for her son Jesus when she made the difficult and risky journey to Egypt at night, soon after giving birth. However, unlike Jesus' family, at the end of an arduous and dangerous pilgrimage on the southern border of the United States, most Latin Americans face detention, nativist contempt, family separation, and deportation. Many are immediately returned to their home countries of violence, poverty, and war, where their suffering continues.

Political scientist Niambi Michele Carter reminds us of an American colonial policy analogous to Herod's murderous command to pluck innocent children from their mothers. She recalls that the separation of children from their parents has been a practice of American colonialism for over four hundred years:

> Whether separating enslaved parents from their children in preparation for sale; Native American parents from their children to place them in boarding school to "civilize" them; or the orphan train movement that took the children of the needy and destitute, many of them immigrants, and resettled them in orphanages across the country, America has never been sentimental about maintaining the sanctity of "family" for those deemed to be outsiders in the American body politic.[18]

In recent history, we have seen the inhumane practice of separating children from their families along the US-Mexico border under America's so-called zero tolerance policy toward unauthorized border crossings. "A voice is heard in Ramah, weeping and great mourning, Rachel weeping for her children and refusing to be comforted." This poetic expression in Jeremiah 31:15 depicts the agonizing pain of the colonized after the invasion of the

Babylonian Empire. Matthew quotes this verse to reference the traumatic violence under the Roman Empire. Now we hear Rachel's desperate cry from the Guatemalan Indian woman in the poem, "Only Say the Word." She cries out under the weight of the American Empire that enables the Guatemalan government, itself a remnant of a former Spanish Colonial Empire, like this:

> Our father who art in heaven,
> Hallowed be thy name,
> Thy Kingdom come,
> Thy will be—
> Our father who art in heaven,
> Hallowed be thy name,
> Thy Kingdom
> Come—
> How many times have I said this prayer!
> How many Sundays have the people of Cordero,
> My village, held hands at Mass
> Begging you, Lord, "Líbranos del mal,"
> Deliver us from evil?
> It does not work,
> The prayer does not work.
> The words turn to stone in my mouth.
> I must find new words
> Now, or I will choke.
> I must make a new prayer
> The way a woman makes new soup
> From yesterday's bones.
> If the old prayer tires you, Lord,
> Be patient.
> I will salt and stir my words,
> A brew so bitter,
> You cannot resist forever,
> You will hear, God,

You will answer.

. . . .

Where is our help,
Christ, Messiah,
Born of a woman who made love
With life?
Must strife be our hated spouse,
Beating us?
Come down off that cross!
That thorny crown is heavy,
You have not lifted your head
In 2000 years,
Eyes closed through
Earthquake, hunger, war.
Nails at your hands and feet,
Rusty, bloody.
Your skin, brown and burnt like mine,
But you are numb.
You were once a troublemaker.
Like a woman with a broom
In filthy house,
You whipped the temple clean
Of greedy men.
Hungry, you picked corn
From another man's fields.
Thirsty, you turned water into wine.
Come down off that cross:
Or we'll call on our old gods,
Give us this day our daily breath,
Deliver us from mad men's claws.[19]

Rachel's cry both in this poem and in Matthew's account mutually correlate and help us imagine the suffering and pain of colonized women, past and present. Like the woman in the poem, the women in Matthew's account must have cried, not simply to grieve the loss of their children, but, like the later victims of the Holocaust, in protest against God, shouting, "It is You who will be judged today! Your children are suffering, and You let it happen! They are hungry, they are ill, they are persecuted and even massacred, and You watch in silence!"[20] Rabbi Ariel Burger states in his memoir *Witness* that this cry of indignation is "the most authentic expression of faith, for it is a testimony to our belief—in spite of what we see—that God is just. And even if God is not, we shall still demand justice."[21]

What then is God's response to these cries? In the Matthean story, Herod is not able to kill all the baby boys. Instead, through divine intervention, Jesus is able to flee this evil and arrive safely in Egypt as a political refugee. The colonial agent Herod cannot win against God; the colonial power of violence cannot rule over God's plan of salvation. God suffers with those who suffer, both in the colonial and postcolonial worlds, and is doing something new for them by planting a mustard seed of "hope against hope" in and through Jesus.

In the Gospel of Matthew, the survival of Jesus as a political refugee is the germination stage of the new chapter of God's plan for human salvation. What then is the condition of the soil in which the seed of hope is planted? Matthew is silent about the migrant life of Jesus' family in Egypt and leaves space for our postcolonial imagination. The Polish sociologist and philosopher, Zygmunt Bauman, informs us that refugees are regarded as "the very embodiment of human waste with no useful function to play in the land of their arrival and temporary stay."[22] Hence, they are treated as strangers, "troublesome, annoying, unwanted," and "inadmissible."[23]

Moreover, according to our own current immigration policy, Jesus' family is undocumented and without legal protection. Was Egypt hospitable in providing them with livable shelter, or were they at risk of family separation and deportation? Was Joseph able to find a job to support his family despite his status as an undocumented migrant? Did they go through culture shock in the new environment of Egyptian culture and language, or did they perhaps live in a ghettoized Jewish community there? Perhaps they were moved to a dumping ground in a remote area. Egypt might not have been an ideal place for refugees. Yet the story says that Mary and Joseph were at least able to protect their baby from the sword until returning to their home country after Herod's death. And so the new beginning of God's salvation is inaugurated in Egypt, once the place of imperial power that oppressed the ancestors of the Israelites. How ironic!

Reading the story of Jesus' escape to Egypt from a postcolonial feminist perspective is a way of reading the text "in front of it," to use Paul Ricouer's term,[24] where the meaning is generated by the reciprocal interaction between the words and the reader's experience and imagination. Such a reading leads us to understand that genuine comfort for the colonized comes from God's hidden activity "to make and keep human life human"[25]—and in ways that exceed our expectations.

Jesus as Postcolonial Child

A Eurocentric colonial reading understands Jesus' escape to Egypt as a manifestation of his divine Sonship. It is worth noting that, as Carter reminds us, the term son or child used for the relationship between God and Jesus in the New Testament does not mean that Jesus is metaphysically divine. Instead, it signifies his "faithful relationship" with God and his "significant function or role in God's salvific purposes" as "God's agent."[26] Thus, as I explained in chapter 1, Jesus' identity is defined by his role in the story, as recognized by the one who intends to speak of it. If Jesus is recognized as the Son of God, it is because of his role as the agent in God's salvific plan, that is, as the mustard seed of hope against hope.

Jesus functioning as God's agent in Matthew's account mirrors the role of children forced to leave their countries by colonial and neocolonial powers, who then reflexively recognize their own identity as God's agents. Those held up at the US-Mexico border by walls, barbed wire, and armed guards are not an obstacle or a trouble. In God's blueprint, found in Jesus, they have the potential to become divine agents who will carry out the salvific plan of God for the world. At this point, Jesus is the image of a postcolonial child.

Jesus' identity as a postcolonial child is a metaphor for a new mode of being for those living in a colonial and postcolonial environment and provides a model for a postcolonial way of living. Jesus' identity as a postcolonial child is good news, not only for the victims, but also for all who live in our neo- and postcolonial world. For, as Letty Russell affirms, "We are all postcolonial subjects continually affected by the history and ongoing economic, religious, cultural, and political implications of colonialism, albeit in very different ways."[27] As a postcolonial child, Jesus calls us to live out as God's agents, as seeds of hope. Perhaps, those born with the privilege of US citizenship may not be comfortable hearing about the oppressive power of *Pax Americana* and might be uninterested in a sermon on Jesus as a political refugee. Nevertheless, preaching Jesus as a postcolonial child can help people redefine their identity in line with their significant function or role in God's salvific purposes, and such preaching is a call to live out life as God's agents for these particular times.

Therefore, the postcolonial feminist reading of the story of Jesus' escape to Egypt leads us to realize that it is a "dangerous memory" of the Christian community. Just as Johann Baptist Metz considers Jesus' crucifixion and resurrection a dangerous memory in his book, Faith in History and Society,[28] this story of incarnation is also a dangerous memory, because it is a memory of God's initiative in breaking the status quo from the margins, from the camps of migrants, refugees, and asylum seekers. To preach Jesus as a postcolonial child is to preach this dangerous memory with its power to turn the present world upside down, to unveil the destructive power of colonial imperialism that prevails in our neo- and postcolonial world, and to revitalize it with the hope in Jesus, the symbol of all postcolonial children. In this sense, preaching Jesus as a postcolonial child is a political act that transmits the dangerous memory of God's incarnation in Jesus Christ to both victims and the privileged in Pax Americana and calls us all to God's salvific plan of reconciliation.

The theological term "reconciliation" does not mean "politeness or a reward for sincere apology."[29] Instead, as practical theologians Herbert Anderson and Edward Foley explain in Mighty Stories, Dangerous Rituals, it is "a way of healing broken relationships and restoring people and communities shattered by violence."[30] It is an ongoing process between victims and victimizers with many moments, allowing time for repairing and healing the hurt "without forgetting the harm."[31] As Anderson and Foley note, "human living with the characteristics of embracing contradiction, honoring the other, showing hospitality to strangers and being surprised by grace"[32] involves participating in actualizing reconciliation. Therefore, reconciliation is an impossible possibility. It is an "eschatological possibility" or a gift of God from God's promise.[33]

Homiletical Strategies

How might preaching fulfill the dual goal of resistance and reconciliation? I suggest that a postcolonial approach to preaching should appeal to the hearts of the listeners through both the cognitive functions of memory and the emotive functions of art.

As Walter Brueggemann sharply notes in his book, *Tenacious Solidarity*, as the beneficiaries of *Pax Americana*, most European American Christians are living in a "self-sufficient affluence" that produces "amnesia."[34] They conveniently forget their ancestors' histories of migration and regard contemporary migrants as an unpleasant interruption. When the *Mayflower* anchored at Cape Cod in 1620, the Pilgrims were strangers to the Native Americans. For over 250 years, before the first federal immigration law was declared in 1875, open-border policies welcomed these strangers. Although their journey of migration and adjustment in a new land was painful, anyone who made an exodus to escape oppression, violence, and poverty could move to the United States and start a new life, conduct a business, serve in the military, and pay taxes. However, according to a survey conducted by the Public Religion Research Institute in 2019, a majority of the members of white Christian churches are in a state of amnesia, with 67 percent of white evangelicals who participated in the survey supporting the building of the border wall and 52 percent of mainline Protestants. In such a context, preaching on the image of Jesus as a political refugee could refresh people's personal and collective memories that all American citizens are either immigrants or the descendants of immigrants.

Moreover, preaching Jesus as a postcolonial child can remind people that hospitality is one of the main responsibilities of a Christian. Hospitality, along with the command to love strangers in both Testaments, is not "a form of charity or entertainment." As Russell insists in *Just Hospitality*, it must be "a form of partnership with the ones we call 'other.'"[35] Preaching hospitality as partnership addresses issues of white supremacy, and it decolonizes listeners' minds by rejecting that imperial idea and providing an opportunity to repent "the cultural sin of self-superiority and domination of others."[36] Ethicist Miguel de la Torre further reminds us that the practice of hospitality performed as an act of charity without taking seriously "the consequences of colonialism" and "the responsibility of restitution" covers up "deep-rooted injustices" involved in the issue of migration.[37]

While the cognitive functions of memory play a significant role in redefining who we are, the emotive functions of art complete preaching by inspiring listeners to participate in the process of reconciliation. Preaching is, in essence, a work that demands the preacher's artistic sense and skills. A postcolonial approach to preaching can be rendered more artistic by coordinating material from the audio-visual arts with words. Music, visual art, film, and poetry that present a postcolonial point of view can stretch listeners' imaginations beyond their limited experiences of past and present, and in so doing, create empathy with the other.

For example, although the story of Jesus' escape to Egypt has been painted by numerous artists, most of the results mitigate the fear and risk conveyed in the story by portraying Jesus' family as white, middle-class people riding a horse or a donkey under the guidance of an angel. In complete contrast, a couple of years ago, a student forwarded me a painting depicting Jesus' family as a contemporary Latin American migrants in blue jeans, crossing a wilderness on foot, with a baby wrapped in a cloth on his mother's bosom. If this picture were to be presented in preaching, it would open listeners' eyes and hearts to imagining the biblical story in a totally different way. Clips from documentary films or movies on forced migration could also be used. For example, the documentary, "Trails of Hope and Terror," produced by Vincent De la Torre, provides information about the history and present situation of Latin American migrants through interviews with a good number of witnesses.[38] Such witnesses could even be invited to preaching events to offer their stories as co-preachers. Poems, like "Only Say the Word" that I shared above, are also powerful for reflecting on the real lives of the victims of Western colonial imperialism.

Finally, the song, "Star-Child," released in 1994,[39] could be a postcolonial song of Christmas. While most Western Christmas music is either sentimental or cheerful, this song, with words by Shirley Murry and music by Carlton Young, makes us think about who Jesus really is. It sings of children in the margins of our postcolonial world as "Street child, beat child, no place left to go, hurt child, used child, no one wants to know," and of Jesus as the symbol of hope: "Hope for peace Child, God's stupendous sign, down-to-earth Child, Star of stars that shine," with the refrain, "this year, this year, let the day arrive when Christmas comes for everyone, everyone alive!"

These are just a few ideas for using art when preaching Jesus as a postcolonial child. Used effectively in a sermon, such creativity can narrow the gap between victims and the privileged in *Pax Americana* and inspire us all to respond to the ethical question, "As the church of Jesus Christ, what must we do for reconciliation and healing?"

CHAPTER 4

Preaching Jesus as Postcolonial Body

ONE OF THE MOST COMPELLING TASKS FOR POSTCOLONIAL preaching is to decolonize traditional interpretations of biblical texts. European Christianity has often interpreted biblical passages to justify Western colonial domination and maintain the status quo. Consciously or unconsciously, marginalized voices and images of liberation and justice in the Bible have been erased, ignored, or distorted. Preaching from a postcolonial perspective means decolonizing the messages based on this sort of biblical interpretation and reinterpreting the gospel of Jesus Christ from the point of view of the colonized. The colonized then become conversational partners in the hermeneutical process of reclaiming the Christian gospel, and their lived experiences form crucial components of new images of Jesus Christ appropriate for our neo- and postcolonial world.

This chapter seeks to reclaim the Easter message by reading chapter 20 of the Gospel of John from a postcolonial perspective. The first section critically examines Easter messages in general, as preached based on the traditional imperialist reading of the text. The second section interprets John 20 through a postcolonial cultural reading. It uses empire studies and postcolonial biblical criticism to decolonize the traditional imperialist interpretation of the text. The third section proposes a new image of Jesus as a postcolonial body, and suggests the profound theological meaning of reconciliation in dialogue with the African American and Native American colonial experiences. The last section offers strategies for preaching Jesus as a postcolonial body: the use of the optative mood, an interpathic approach, and the homiletical movement from lament to hope.

THE RISEN JESUS AND EASTER MESSAGES

The narrative of Jesus' resurrection is found in all four Gospels. While each Gospel describes this event in a unique way, John details it the most. Chapter 20 of his Gospel is comprised of four scenes—the empty tomb (vv. 1–10), Mary Magdalene's encounter with the risen Jesus (vv. 11–18), Jesus' appearance to the disciples (vv. 19–23), and Jesus' appearance to Thomas (vv. 24–29)—plus a conclusion stating that the purpose of the Gospel is for readers to believe Jesus is the Messiah, the Son of God (vv. 30–31). It is no wonder the *Revised Common Lectionary* covers the entire chapter over two consecutive Sundays—Easter Sunday (20:1–18) and the Second Sunday of Easter (20:19–31)—in all three years of Years A, B, and C.

According to theologian Shelly Rambo's review, the traditional reading of this chapter focuses on belief in the risen Jesus. His resurrected body is conceived as flawless and glorious and represents his perfect divinity. Easter sermons based on this traditional interpretation emphasize the triumph and glory of the risen Jesus, who is divine, and exhort listeners to believe in the resurrection that they might also have a glorious spiritual body in the afterlife.[1] Rambo illustrates the point with John Calvin's commentary on John 20, in which he emphasizes the significance of faith in the risen Christ and denounces Mary Magdalene, Peter, Thomas, and other disciples for being in a "state of confusion," and for the "carnal stupidity" that prevents them from believing in the resurrection.[2]

For Calvin, Jesus' resurrected body, which represents his divinity, is "glorious" and "unmarked by human limitation."[3] Calvin understands that the faith in this divinity comes from Christ's self-revelation because that faith "does not consist in seeing what is before us, but penetrates to the very heavens, so as to believe the things which are hidden from the human senses."[4] Consequently, Calvin depicts Thomas, who wants to touch Jesus' body, as "a lazy, reluctant, obstinate disciple, one who, contrary to the vision of him as the intellectual, is 'dull of apprehension.'"[5] The only reason the risen Jesus permits Thomas to touch his scars, Calvin explains, is because God is accommodating the removal of his doubt. Moreover, the reason Jesus prohibits Mary Magdalene from touching his body is because she is not seeking to increase her faith in his resurrection, but "keep him here on earth."[6]

Furthermore, Calvin interprets the risen Jesus' commission to his disciples—"If you forgive the sins of any, they are forgiven them; if you retain the sins of any, they are retained" (v. 23)—as the privilege of those with faith in the resurrection, and reminds readers that "the principle purpose of the preaching of the gospel" is to have "men [sic] be reconciled to God by the free remission."[7] For Calvin, reconciliation by free remission means personal spiritual salvation. Along with other sixteenth-century reformers, he understands that to know that the risen Jesus is "the Messiah and the Son of God" (v. 31) is possible only by faith, and this faith comes not from "the sensuality of touch"[8] but from "hearing the word and responding to it."[9]

Out of this emphasis on the significance of hearing the word, preaching became the center of Protestant worship, while belief in the resurrection of Jesus became the core message of Christianity. Hence, Easter worship celebrated the divinity of Jesus manifested in the triumph and glory of the risen Christ, and in their Easter sermons, preachers used the story of the "doubting Thomas" (vv. 24–29) as "a cautionary tale to persons of faith."[10]

It is noteworthy that Calvin disregards the scars in the body of the risen Jesus, mentioning them only in a passing reference. As Rambo rightly indicates, this reading strategy goes back to the fourth-century Christological controversy in the Roman Empire between Roman Catholicism and Arianism.[11] While the Catholic belief was that Jesus was fully human and fully divine and that all three persons of the Holy Trinity were formed from the same substance (*homoousios*), Arius insisted on the humanity of the Christ, by arguing that Jesus was not God in nature, and that the persons of the Holy Trinity shared a similar substance (*homoiousios*), but were separate. Arius strengthened his position by arguing that "although Christ is a glorified creature, he is still a creature, evidenced by the marks on this flesh."[12] The conflict between Catholic and Arian Christianity in the Roman Empire continued until Arianism was officially condemned at the Council of Chalcedon in 451 CE, under the leadership of the Roman emperor.

The Council of Chalcedon is representative of the collusive relation between the Roman Empire and Christianity. Since the conversion of Emperor Constantine I in 312 CE, Christian believers largely had religious freedom. Christians were no longer persecuted, and Christianity became the official religion of the Empire, moving its worship spaces from houses to Roman basilicas. The cost of this freedom, however, was to make Jesus the protector of the Roman Empire.[13] Jesus of Nazareth was granted the title "Son of God,"[14] an appellation given to Roman emperors who claimed their origin from a divine figure, identified as the Sun, a Conqueror who safeguarded the peace of the Empire.[15] The price for the elevation of Christianity was that the Christian church had to revise its historical memory of Jesus of Nazareth. It replaced his thorny crown with a golden one and erased the marks of the Roman imperial violence from his risen body in order to present his divine kingship to the Romans. This collusive relation between the Christian Church and the Roman Empire was evident at the Council of Chalcedon. The victory of the institutional

Roman church at the Council paved the way for the emperor to maintain the unity of the Eastern Roman Empire. At the same time, Marcian, emperor and head of the church, acknowledged the authority of Pope Leo I, by granting him primacy in the episcopate of the Christian faith.[16]

Calvin's reading of John 20, "Belief in the resurrection is belief in the full divinity of Christ,"[17] affirms the Chalcedonian Creed, which was backed up by the Roman Empire. It thus resonates with the tradition of the Roman imperialist interpretation, something that becomes clear if we compare Calvin's view with that of St. Augustine's in the fifth century. In his commentary, Augustine also denounces Thomas' request to touch the marks on Jesus' body as indictive of a lack of faith, and highlights the significance of faith in the divinity of Jesus. Furthermore, he warns that the five senses of the body—sight, hearing, smell, taste, and touch—should not be an impediment to belief in the risen Christ. The only reason for the risen Jesus to keep his scars, says Augustine, is so that "they might be touched by the doubting Apostle and the wounds of his heart be healed." Nevertheless, the Lord Jesus could have risen again without the scars.[18]

This traditional imperialist reading of John 20 reflects a European Christian theological preoccupation with seeing Jesus' death as the atonement for the moral and religious sins of individual believers, and his resurrection as the gift of God that promises them the remission of those sins.[19] Throughout the Reformation and Enlightenment, Christianity became more privatized and spiritualized, often detached from core political and societal institutions.[20] As a consequence, Jesus' crucifixion and resurrection have been preached as apolitical and ahistorical events promising personal salvation, i.e., life after death. Many churches in the United States have been nurtured by this kind of message and thus fail to preach a theologically appropriate and culturally relevant Easter message to and for those who are living in our neo- and postcolonial contexts. With such a traditional imperialist slant, the Easter message closes any possibilities of healing to those who suffer under Western colonial and neocolonial imperialism, and impedes reconciliation between colonizers and colonized of both past and present.

A Postcolonial Cultural Reading

What then might the Easter message be like if we were to interpret John 20 through a postcolonial lens? How might it be different from the traditional message? A postcolonial cultural reading helps preachers create a meaning for the text that is completely different from the traditional reading, and hence more relevant to our contemporary listeners. Such an approach employs three reading strategies. First, a postcolonial cultural reading takes the Roman colonial imperialism as the key factor in interpreting John 20 and situates the text in the cultural context of the Roman Empire. While the traditional imperialist reading pays little attention to the historical and cultural setting of the resurrection narrative and renders the Roman Empire invisible, contemporary biblical scholarship, focused on empire studies and postcolonial biblical criticism, provides ample information about the first-century environment where Jesus and his followers—and later John's original audience—lived as the colonized.

The colonized under Roman rule experienced brutal violence daily, not only physically but also mentally, psychologically, economically, and culturally. In addition to these daily experiences, Jesus' disciples witnessed the horrific scene of their teacher's crucifixion. As biblical scholar Richard Horsley explains, crucifixion was a powerful symbol of Roman rule, with thousands of colonized Judeans executed on crosses in order to intimidate the surviving populace into acquiescence with the Roman colonial order.[21] In John 20, Mary Magdalene, Thomas, and the other disciples having witnessed Jesus' crucifixion are traumatized with shock, fear, and doubt. Mary's frantic search for the lost body of Jesus and her failure to recognize his voice (vv. 11–15); the disciples' locking the doors out of fear (v. 19); and Thomas's doubt about the presence of the risen Jesus (vv. 24–29) are all symptomatic reactions to their post-traumatic colonial stress disorder. Thus, this cultural reading understands Mary Magdalene's anxiety, the disciples' fear, and Thomas's doubt, not as something blameworthy, as the traditional imperialist reading would have it, but as symptoms of a trauma that needs to be healed. In this cultural context, the event of Jesus' resurrection replaces their traumatic memory of Rome's brutal terrorism. In encountering the risen Jesus, they witness God's life-giving power against the colonial power of violence, and they experience healing that frees them from anxiety, fear, and doubt. Therefore, reading the resurrection narrative in John 20 through a postcolonial cultural lens convinces us that "the Empire does not have the final word!"[22]

The second strategy for a postcolonial cultural reading is concerned with the original audience of the text. While most interpretive methods for preaching focus on the characters in the biblical text and create meaning by identifying them with contemporary listeners through analogical imagination, a postcolonial cultural reading is interested in the original historical audience of the text, as well as the biblical characters, and investigates these cultural environments in a comparison between those of the original audience and those of contemporary listeners through "cultural intertextuality."[23] Cultural intertextuality means reading the Bible in parallel with other historical, cultural, and religious literature to gather information about the cultural environments of the biblical and the early church periods.

For whom, then, did John write his Gospel? What motivated him to do so? There is no historical record indicating who John's audience was, and so Warren Carter investigates the question through cultural intertextuality.[24] In dialogue with other Jewish and Greco-Roman literature written during the first century, and along with other prominent New Testament scholars, he concludes that John's audience was the diaspora communities of

"Jesus-believers" who were living in Ephesus, the center of the Roman Empire in the East, after the defeat and destruction of Jerusalem and its temple in 70 AD.[25] Thus, like other stories in the Gospel of John, the resurrection narrative in chapter 20 is not a factual historical record based on the "immediate memory or retention" of the original witnesses of Jesus' resurrection. It is, rather, a "secondary memory (recollection) or reproduction"[26] written more than half a century later when the immediate memory had faded. As philosopher and sociologist Maurice Halbwachs insists, it is "based more on dogma than on actual testimony."[27]

According to Carter's historical and cultural hypothesis, the lives of Jesus-believers and the Jewish synagogue communities in Ephesus had become "too accommodated, too comfortable,"[28] as a result of negotiating "the political, economic, and social dimensions of everyday, material, physical life under Rome's rule,"[29] to resist its oppressive colonial realities. The Gospel was thus intended to guide those who were struggling daily over the issue of negotiation with Roman imperial power. It reminds its readers of Jesus' challenge to and his conflict with the Roman authorities, and presents the reign of God as the alternative to the Roman Empire.[30]

The information about John's original audience shows us that his audience in Ephesus and our listeners in the United States are in similar situations. Just as the former lived in negotiation with the imperial colonial culture of the *Pax Romana*, so too do the latter live in the culture of the *Pax Americana*. A postcolonial cultural reading encourages preachers to read the text standing in the shoes of both audiences, and to engage with the marginalized and suppressed voices of the colonized in both biblical times and the present.

The third strategy for a postcolonial cultural reading for preaching is to interpret the symbols, signs, and stories in the text through a postcolonial imagination. The Gospel of John does not have an account of the transfiguration. Instead, it says that

Jesus' crucified body is transfigured and glorified without obliterating the marks of suffering and death. When we read John 20 through a postcolonial lens, our imagination zooms in to his bodily presence. When he appears to Mary Magdalene (vv. 1–18), the disciples (vv. 19–23), and to Thomas and the other disciples (vv. 24–29), his presence is not spiritualized, but somatic, for he carries the scars from his crucifixion. Jesus' bodily presence is the consistent theme throughout John's Gospels. As Carter explains, John presents who Jesus is and what he is about through his somatic and communal presence: healing sick bodies, feeding the hungry, building a community of followers, and dying from public physical torture on the cross.[31]

John depicts even Jesus' resurrection as a bodily presence. According to John's description, the body of the risen Jesus is not splendid or perfect, but has the scars of the wounds caused by imperial violence (vv. 20, 27). Jesus' bodily presence embracing these scars symbolizes a condition of healing and reconciliation. His scars reveal that the wounds he suffered on the cross are healed. He now remembers the past without pain and with the capacity to reconcile with those who harmed him by forgiving their sins. As the symbol of healing and reconciliation, the risen Jesus calls his disciples to come out of the locked room (vv. 11–23), to go into the world of the Roman colonial culture, to equip themselves with the power of the Holy Spirit, and to work for healing and reconciliation by forgiving the sins of the colonizers (vv. 19–21). Therefore, the scars in the body of the risen Jesus exist not merely to help the disciples believe in his resurrection, but have a profound theological meaning in themselves as the sign of healing and reconciliation.

The bodily presence of Jesus, risen and scarred, not only reminds the disciples of the past, but also promises them "life in his name" (v. 31), or eternal life amid the deadly violence of the Empire. The traditional imperialist reading privatizes "life in his name" by interpreting it as a future-oriented eschatological life, i.e., life after death, given as a reward to those who believe in him as Savior. However, Carter notes that the original meaning of the word *aiōnion* in Greek—which has been translated into the English term "eternal" or "everlasting"—means not "after" but "of" the age or "of" the era. Thus, the accurate meaning of eternal or everlasting life in the Gospel of John is "life of the age,"[32] It is proleptic eschatological life that is not solely a future event, but is already present in continuity and transformation (cf. 1 Cor 15).[33]

Carter further explains that belief in the bodily resurrection is uniquely Jewish, in that it emerged from "Jewish negotiations of imperial power."[34] It is the political act "whereby God's faithful power extended beyond death to redress acts of injustice."[35] In this sense, the narrative of the bodily presence of Jesus is a counter narrative to the imperial narrative which emphasizes that the Empire has the final word. When from this postcolonial cultural perspective we read Thomas's confession, "my Lord, my God" (v. 28), which takes a climactic place in the chapter, it is not a mere statement of personal faith. It is instead a profound theological claim to the world that God is sovereign over all the empires in human history, including the Roman and the American Empires.

Jesus as Postcolonial Body

A postcolonial cultural reading of John 20 presents the image of the risen Jesus as a bodily presence with the scars of his colonial wounds. Unlike the traditional imperialist reading, the image is neither splendid nor flawless. But it is beautiful because it embraces the dehumanized broken body in the divine presence and symbolizes healing and reconciliation. This new image of Jesus represents a postcolonial body. It goes through and beyond the suffering and death caused by colonial violence and opens possibilities of healing and reconciliation—a new humanity in a state of peace. In other words, Jesus' dehumanized body is transfigured into a postcolonial presence that overcomes the power of death and presents the life-giving power of God to the world for all, both the colonized and colonizers.

In this sense, preaching the risen Jesus as a postcolonial body reproduces a "countermemory."[36] According to Michel Foucault, a counter memory opposes traditional memory or traditional history. It is "a transformation of history into a totally different form of time."[37] As homiletician John McClure elaborates, a counter memory comes from "looking at the inscription of history on the marginalized body and reading backward to the 'countless lost events' that were never to become monuments around which to organize collective memory."[38] As a recollection of lost memories in history, the counter memory comes from listening to historically marginalized people and reconstructing memory from their point of view. Thus, preaching a countermemory is possible when preachers exit the traditional imperialist account "in order to find its memory of what is otherwise."[39]

Most colonized people, both past and present, have lived as "historically marginalized people," negatively impacted by the trauma of colonialism and imperialism. Native Americans, for example, had lived in North America for an approximately fourteen thousand years, with an estimated population of eighteen million when the European colonists arrived. Today, just over five million Native Americans remain.[40] European colonialism, along with the incentives of Christian mission, decimated the great multitudes of these people through "land theft, armed removal and relocation, forced breakup of families, the outlawing of Indigenous religion, bureaucratic policies of extermination, assimilation and racism, [and] rape of the land," not to mention exposure to various European diseases, such as mumps, measles, and chicken pox that accompanied the settlers.[41]

This terrorism was supported by the Doctrine of Discovery, notions of Manifest Destiny, a belief in American Exceptionalism, and the Great Commission (Matthew 28:18–20). It is justified in the following statement from the former US secretary of state, Henry Clay, in 1825:

> There was never a full-blooded Indian who took to civilization. It is not in their nature. They are destined to extinction.... I do not think they are, as a race, worth preserving. I consider them as essentially inferior to the Anglo-Saxon race which is now taking their place on this continent.... [T]heir disappearance from the human family will be no great loss to the world.[42]

Native American theologian Randy Woodley informs us that the deadly impact of this colonial history of ethnic cleansing and genocide continues among Native Americans in the form of "post-colonial stress disorder (PCSD)," which is "intergenerational trauma as a result of the colonial plague."[43]

Endorsed by the Christian Church, European colonialism has also destroyed "the physical Black body, and thus Black humanity."[44] From the Middle Passage (the journey from Africa to the Americas by slave ships) and through enslavement, Black bodies were considered "the property, of production, of reproduction, of sexual violence."[45] Black female bodies, in particular, have been mistreated and have unjustly suffered, as English professor Hortense J. Spillers writes:

> One of the most poignant aspects of William Goodell's contemporaneous study of the North American slave codes gives definitive expression to the tortures and instruments of captivity. Reporting an instance of Jonathan Edwards's observations on the tortures of enslavement, Goodell narrates: "The smack of the whip is all day long in the ears of those who are on the plantation, or in the vicinity; and it is used with such dexterity and severity as not only to lacerate the skin, but to tear out small portions of the flesh at almost every stake." The anatomical specifications of rupture, of altered human tissue, take on the objective description of laboratory prose—eyes beaten out,

arms, backs, skulls branded, a left jaw, a right ankle, punctured; teeth missing, as the calculated work of iron, whips, chains, knives, the canine patrol, the bullet. . . . A female body strung from a tree limb, or bleeding from the breast on any given day of field work because the "overseer," standing the length of a whip, has popped her flesh open, adds a lexical and living dimension to the narratives of women in culture and society.[46]

Resmaa Menakem, an African American psychotherapist, further explains that such hardships of African Americans are ongoing experiences:

> Over 300 years, the Black body in America has been systematically brutalized, mutilated, murdered, abused, controlled, raped, objectified, and demonized by guns, whips, chains, and manacles; shootings, lynchings, and rape; by laws, policies, social norms, and codes of behavior; and by images and concepts. For centuries, trauma upon trauma compounded.[47]

More precisely, when the first Jim Crow laws were enacted in 1877, nearly 3,500 Black bodies were lynched.[48] Since the "War on Drugs" began in the early 1980s, almost 40 percent of people incarcerated for drug law violations have been Black, even though Blacks make up only about 13 percent of the country's population.[49] And police regularly pull over Black drivers simply because they are Black. Because of these "everyday stressors, micro-aggressions, and a lack of regard,"[50] many African Americans have collective and communal experiences of trauma, further supported by symptomatic evidence of "post-traumatic stress disorder (PTSD),[51] learning disabilities, depression and anxiety, diabetes, high blood pressure, and other physical and emotional ailments."[52]

After recalling these neglected collective memories of the colonized people, the next step in preaching Jesus as a postcolonial body is to reflect on possibilities of healing and reconciliation through an imagination based on the postcolonial cultural reading of the text. As theologian Curtis Paul DeYoung argues, reconciliation is often misunderstood as "assimilation, appeasement, a passive peace, a unity without cost, and maintaining power with only cosmetic changes."[53] Theologian Willie James Jennings also warns that the theological term reconciliation has been misused as an "ideological tool" or "idealist claim" and that "most Christians are [not] ready to imagine reconciliation."[54] Nevertheless, reconciliation has a theologically profound meaning, because it is God's purpose for humanity as represented in the body of the risen Jesus. DeYoung explains that the term reconciliation translates the word, *katallassō*, which literally means "to change or exchange." Thus, "when we are 'reconciled,' we exchange places 'with the other,' and [are] in solidarity with rather than against 'the other.'" In other words, reconciliation is "a process that causes us to overcome alienation through identification and in solidarity with 'the other,' thus making peace and restoring relationships,"[55] by engaging at the heart of the struggle for justice in the world. Thus, reconciliation between the colonized and colonizers means a process aimed at ending colonialism and imperialism.

Is reconciliation between colonized and colonizers possible? Can imperial colonialism cease to exist in the world? Considering that the prerequisite for reconciliation is forgiveness, can the colonized forgive the colonizers' sins—the genocides, lynchings, slavery, rapes, the extraction of natural and human resources, and the intergenerational trauma caused by these sins? A postcolonial cultural reading of John 20 answers this question, not from the human point of view, but from God's point of view, for God has already initiated this process by raising Jesus from the dead. His bodily resurrection bears witness to the lordship of God over the Roman emperors; the scars in his glorified body are signs of reconciliation. Jesus' crucifixion embodies a reality of the colonial sin—imperial violence and dehumanization—too horrendous to be humanly forgivable. Nevertheless, those who believe in the risen Jesus have the capacity to forgive and reconcile with the colonizers through the intervention of the Holy Spirit (vv. 22–23).

Paul Ricoeur reflects on the possibility of forgiveness of sins and understands forgiveness as a gift of the Holy Spirit, just as John's Gospel does:

> [A]type of cruelty, of baseness, of extreme inequality in social conditions distresses me without my being able to name the norms violated. . . . It makes forgiving difficult, not easy, but not impossible. . . . "There is forgiveness." . . . This voice [is] a voice from above. . . . It is a silent voice but not a mute one. Silent, because there is no clamor of what rages; not mute, because not deprived of speech. An appropriated discourse is in fact dedicated to it, the hymn. A discourse of praise and celebration. It says: *il y a, es gibt,* there is . . . forgiveness—the form of the universal designating *illéité* [otherness]. For the hymn has no need to say who forgives and to whom forgiveness is directed. There is forgiveness as there is joy, as there is wisdom, extravagance, love. Love, precisely. Forgiveness belongs to the same family. How could one not evoke the hymn to love proclaimed by Saint Paul in the First Epistle to the Corinthians? But, attention: what the hymn names is not someone, . . . but a "spiritual gift—a "charisma"—grounded by the Holy Spirit. . . . Now if love excuses everything, this everything includes the unforgivable. . . . [Forgiveness] is unconditional, it is without exception and without restriction. It does not presuppose a request for forgiveness.[56]

For Ricoeur, forgiveness is a spiritual gift, much like unconditional love. He expounds on this in terms of the commandment to love our enemies and makes an interesting point:

> The commandment to love one's enemies begins by breaking the rule of reciprocity and requiring the extraordinary. Faithful to the gospel rhetoric of hyperbole, according to this commandment the only gift that is justified is that one given to

the enemy, from whom, by hypothesis, one expects nothing in return. But, precisely, the hypothesis is false: what one expects from love is that it will convert the enemy into a friend.[57]

Like love, forgiveness as a spiritual gift grounded by the Holy Spirit, can convert enemies into friends, and friendship is the true state of reconciliation between colonized and colonizers. When the victims of colonialism and imperialism live as a postcolonial body, as spiritual beings, they can embrace their enemies by forgiving their sins in love and building friendship with them. Native American theologian Randy Woodley also sees the possibility of forgiveness from a Native American perspective on humanity:

> In many of our Native American traditions, we have a prayer that often goes something like, "Have pity/understanding on me Creator and remember, I am just a human being." The idea behind this prayer is that perfection is the enemy of attainment. We are all simply human beings, imperfect but learning from our mistakes. . . . That seems to be one of our greatest theological statements—we're just human beings, and so we also can forgive other human beings.[58]

If the colonized initiate reconciliation by forgiving colonial sins, what must colonizers do, in turn, to be reconciled with the colonized? DeYoung states that "reconciliation for the powerful and privileged means trusting those who have lived under oppression and even following their lead in becoming one new humanity."[59] In other words, reconciliation is possible when colonizers live a new life as a postcolonial body by liberating themselves from their "nonlegitimate identity of superiority and [its] privileges."[60] How might this happen? Again, by the intervention of the Holy Spirit. Preachers need to participate in this transforming work of the Holy Spirit by inspiring listeners with the countermemory of the risen Jesus, and by inviting them to participate in God's purpose of reconciliation by living as a postcolonial body.

Preachers who have never been in the situation of the colonized readily spiritualize the resurrection account in John, and their sermons emphasize salvation after death through the belief in the risen Christ, in the manner of traditional imperial reading. Likewise, preachers who belong to a group that has been colonized in the past or in the present also read the text from an individual perspective, and their sermons also tend to emphasize personal salvation through belief in the risen Jesus. By contrast, postcolonial preachers find new ways to understand themselves and their listeners in solidarity with one another and read the bodily presence of the risen Jesus as a symbol of reconciliation. Sermons based on such readings go beyond personal salvation and invite listeners to think together about how they might live as reconcilers or bridge-makers, crossing their racial, ethnic, and social boundaries and exchanging their places with "the other."

Preaching the risen Jesus as a postcolonial body is preaching as countermemory. It goes against the traditional individualistic and spiritualized messages of the risen Christ. Preaching as countermemory challenges the colonized, the colonizers, and their churches to renew their identities by remembering who God in the risen Jesus is and who we are as the Jesus believers. The Easter message that witnesses to the risen Jesus as a postcolonial body is therefore an invitation to God's ongoing work of reconciliation.

Homiletical Strategies

Preaching Jesus as a postcolonial body not only protests the injustices before God and others, but also participates in God's purpose of reconciliation by inviting listeners and their churches to new identities as reconcilers. Just as reconciliation between colonized and colonizers depends on the intervention of the Holy Spirit, so too does preaching Jesus as a postcolonial body. Just as the risen Jesus breathed on his disciples (v. 22), so too do listeners need the divine breath to continue the work he commissioned. When God approaches listeners and they in turn approach God through preaching, the moment of preaching becomes a meeting place or Third Space where the divine Spirit and the human spirit interconnect and generate a new identity of individual listeners and churches as reconcilers. The following four homiletical strategies may help preachers invoke the presence of the Holy Spirit to work for transformation through preaching:

The first homiletical strategy is to use the optative mood. Reconciliation does not happen by issuing an order. Rather, it is a process characterized by anticipation, a wish, a desire, and a hope. Reconciliation is what God hopes for the world, and it is our hope for the wholeness of all God's creatures. We long for God's reign to complete reconciliation—healing, justice, mutuality, and peace. Hence, the most appropriate grammatical mood for preaching Jesus as a postcolonial body is the optative. As Ricoeur defines it, the optative mood is "at equal distance from the indicative of description and the imperative of prescription."[61] In the optative mood, the preacher, on the one hand, longs for God's reign of reconciliation and, on the other, invokes the Holy Spirit to help empower the colonized with the capacity to forgive, and to move the colonizers to be accountable for their colonial sins. In this way, preaching in the optative mood is proleptically eschatological. It underscores the dimensions of both anticipation and projection.

As a concrete example of preaching in the optative mood, homiletician Sarah Travis's idea of crafting a sermon like a piece of contrapuntal music is insightful:

> In music, contrapuntal is a piece of music that has two distinct melodic lines. Perhaps this is a way to think about telling the story of the resurrection in the face of trauma. We tell two stories at the same time: One of a resurrection that has overcome death and one that testifies to the ongoingness of death even in the face of the resurrection.[62]

As Travis's contrapuntal preaching demonstrates, preaching in the optative mood stands between the two worlds. With both feet planted in the actual mess of human life, the preacher proclaims the gospel of reconciliation that the risen Jesus promises. In this sense, preaching Jesus as a postcolonial body is a prayer, "Thy will be done, on earth as it is in heaven."

The second homiletical strategy for creating a Third Space is to use an interpathic approach. In order to fully engage with racially and culturally diverse experiences when preparing a sermon, preachers need to cross their racial and cultural comfort zones and experience others' lives through interpathy. As pastoral theologian and counselor David Augsburger defines it, interpathy is like empathy in the sense that both are ways of understanding another through the imaginative projection of one's own feelings or emotional state onto the other. But unlike empathy, where people share common cultural assumptions, interpathy is the attempt to enter a world of assumptions which are totally different from our own. It is the capacity to see as others see and to see ourselves as others see us. By projecting our own feelings onto the other, interpathy builds bridges between different people with different identities.[63] By suffering with those who suffer and by mourning with those who mourn, preachers search for the presence of the Holy Spirit and bear witness to what God is doing in their lives. By sharing those stories in preaching, the preacher can help listeners learn about the reconciling work of the Holy Spirit in the world and call them and their churches to participate therein as agents of reconciliation.[64]

The third homiletical strategy for invoking the Holy Spirit is to design a sermon with a threefold movement that follows the lead of the Holy Spirit. The first movement is to help listeners be aware of the broken bodies in our neo- and postcolonial world, by witnessing the suffering and pain of colonized people through an interpathic approach. By listening to the colonial oppression and trauma from both biblical times and in the present, listeners can engage with the personal and social trauma colonized people have suffered historically. The second movement of the sermon is to lament with the Holy Spirit. Lamenting here is both to remember the shameful history of colonialism in human history and to mourn our own suffering and the suffering of others. We, as the church, lament on behalf of or alongside others through interpathy, as the Spirit intercedes for us to reconnect with God and with others. To lament is to express profound faith with confidence that God the Spirit will not remain silent, but will act with, through, and for us. The last movement of the sermon is to remind listeners of God's promise in the risen Christ. By preaching the countermemory of the bodily presence of the risen Jesus with his scars, the sermon offers hope for the future and invites listeners to the reconciling work of the Holy Spirit. Through this threefold movement of the sermonic form, the Holy Spirit can work with the preacher to move listeners from lament to hope, from enmity to forgiveness, and from alienation to reconciliation.

Therefore, Easter sermons on the risen Jesus as a postcolonial body can contribute to God's purpose of reconciliation through the intervention of the Holy Spirit. Such sermons can provide new directions for the church and society by evoking a collective imagination to reconstruct our world. As a result, preaching Jesus as a postcolonial body is itself an act of reconciliation, a process of humanization.

CHAPTER 5

Preaching Jesus as Postcolonial Friend

CHRISTIANITY IS PRIMARILY A MISSION-ORIENTED RELIGION. Sharply criticized by postcolonial and other liberation theologians, the mission of Western Christianity has been practiced alongside Western imperial colonialism. If we were to choose the biblical text that has contributed most to the Christian colonialist mission, it would be Matthew 28:16–20, known as the Great Commission. It is the final scene of the Gospel of Matthew, in which the resurrected Jesus meets his eleven disciples on the mountain in Galilee and commissions them to go and make disciples of all nations by baptizing and teaching them.

Postcolonial biblical scholar Musa W. Dube notes that this passage has been used as "an imperialist text—a text that was used to subjugate other races and nations, men as well as women; a text that articulates an ideology of imperialism."[1] Indeed, this text may have encouraged Western Christian churches to missionize non-Christians, and its literal meaning has been the guidepost for missions in partnership with colonialist governments, in order to expand their territories, wealth, and power. Considering this negative impact of the Great Commission, a challenge for preachers is what to do with this text. Should we erase it from the list of sermonic texts? Or should we continue to preach it? If so, what should we preach, and how?

Chapter 5

Lectionary preachers encounter Matthew 28:16–20 every three years. It is the Gospel reading for Trinity Sunday in Year C of the *Revised Common Lectionary*. According to the Christian calendar, the celebration of Easter ends with the Day of Pentecost and is followed by Trinity Sunday, which celebrates the life of the church whose mission is to witness Jesus Christ "to the ends of the earth" (Acts 1:8) until "the end of the age" (Matt. 28:20), in the continuing presence of the risen Jesus. What would it be like if we preached Jesus by reading the Great Commission through a postcolonial lens?

This chapter aims to help preachers critically examine the traditional colonialist interpretation of the Great Commission and its impact on the colonized and to reconsider the nature and function of missional preaching from a postcolonial perspective. The first section examines the intricate relation between the Great Commission and Western colonialism and its impact on preaching. The second section interprets the text through a postcolonial intertextual approach and provides insight into Christian mission as building friendship. The third presents a new image of Jesus as a postcolonial friend and discusses the essence of Christian mission in our neo- and postcolonial world. The last section suggests homiletical strategies for preaching Jesus as a postcolonial friend considering the concept of "meta preaching."

THE GREAT COMMISSION AND THE WESTERN COLONIALIST MISSION

From the burgeoning of the European Christian mission in the fifteenth century and onward, as womanist ethicist Katie Cannon argues in her article, "Christian Imperialism and the Transatlantic Slave Trade,"[2] this Christian mission has been a product of the collusive relationship between Western European countries and their Christian churches. Papal bulls in 1455 and 1493 affirmed that "European nations which 'discovered' land inhabited by Indigenous peoples had a 'right of domination' over those lands and peoples."³ This Doctrine of Discovery was sealed in the Treaty of Tordesillas (1494) in which Pope Alexander VI ratified Portugal and Spain's claims to Africa and allowed their aggressive and ruthless expeditions there under the condition that the governments were responsible for converting the indigenous people to Christianity.⁴

The Doctrine of Discovery originated with the Christian church was based on an imperialist interpretation of the Christian Scriptures, including the Great Commission.

According to Cannon, the Christian interpretation and application of the Great Commission legitimized and supported the transatlantic slave trade. The Christian mission was spurred by the biblical urgency of the *Parousia*, "the quickly approaching, expected hope of the return of Christ as judge to terminate this world order,"⁵ itself based on the Great Commission and was supported by "structured white supremacy ideology."⁶ Missionaries believed that

> whoever is a disciple of Jesus Christ must go into the entire world and "make disciples of all nations, baptizing them in the name of the Father, and the Son, and the Holy Spirit." And since no one knows the exact day or the hour when Jesus will return, these patrons of the governors' trading companies decided that they would enhance their nation's economic, political, and spiritual health by accelerating the spread of Christianity.⁷

The Great Commission, as a convenient rhetorical weapon for deepening the conjunction between evangelism and European colonial expansion, was practiced with a three-step conversion process, as Cannon explains:

> First, invite the king or paramount chief to a meeting. The second step took place at the meeting's end, when the king and the indigenous masses were encouraged to pledge full

submission to Jesus Christ as savior. And finally, if indigenous people refused to forsake the god of their religion and resisted entrusting their lives to the conqueror in the name of Christ, it was not only legal but also an act of faith, a religious duty sanctioned by God, for Christian imperialists to use whatever force was necessary—murder, starvation, rape, disease, physical exhaustion, and slavery in perpetuity—in order to rescue inferior benighted brethren, identified as heathens, savages, infidels, pagans, and enemies of Christ.[8]

The European imperial church acknowledged an ideology of white supremacy ideology that essentialized whites as God's chosen people, "the superior, natural masters, hereditarily pure, glorious, free citizens," and Blacks as "natural slaves, inherently defective, depraved, and inferior" who were "cursed with perpetual servitude."[9] Furthermore, the church approved of the claim that Christian missionaries and colonial expansionists "not only had the right but a vocational responsibility to colonize the lands, bodies, labor, and minds of the rest of the world."[10]

The Great Commission was also the mandate for Protestant missionaries. It became the "Magna Carta of missions" for Protestant churches during the nineteenth and the twentieth centuries when their zeal for overseas missions was at its peak. Dutch neo-Calvinist Abraham Kuyper's lecture on missions, delivered at a mission conference in Amsterdam in 1890, illustrates this. Based on a literal interpretation of the Great Commission, he emphasizes that "[a]ll mission is essentially obedience to God's command; and the content of the message likewise is not an invitation but a commandment, an order. The Lord does not recommend or exhort but mandates."[11] He offers further mission strategies as follows:

> Missions among pagans have four objectives: First, reject their idols; then bring the ministers of the idols to the sacrament of baptism so that they can reveal the church of Christ to their

people; next, link this manifestation of the church with the mother church; and finally, replace the pagan way of life with a Christian form or life-style.[12]

Missionaries and their churches believed that they were ordered by Jesus, their commander, to convert the indigenous people of the Americas, Africa, and Asia to Christianity at any cost. They dedicated all their efforts to increasing the number of converts by whatever means. For example, they translated the Bible into indigenous people's languages and taught it to them. Then, by establishing educational institutions, they imposed Western culture and its worldview on the natives, representing it as superior, condemning indigenous religions as demonic and heathen, and promoting Jesus Christ as Savior.[13] When encountering injustices perpetrated by Western colonialists, such as the trading of human beings and other physical abuses, cultural and religious extermination, and economic exploitation, most missionaries and their institutional churches were silent and thereby complicit with such dehumanization. They overlooked the suffering and pain of the people to whom they were proclaiming the gospel and tried to focus on planting new churches without interfering with the colonialist leaders.[14]

Many Protestant churches of the United States during the nineteenth and the twentieth centuries were no exception. According to theologian Mayra Rivera, Puerto Rico is one of the victims of the tangled relationship between US imperialism and Christian mission. American missionaries contributed to the US invasion of occupation of Puerto Rico in 1898 by following the directives of Robert McLean, who served as a missionary there: "To know the mind of God is the first requisite of the missionary, but next to that he must come to knowledge of the mind of the people over whom he shall be placed by the Holy Spirit."[15] Here, explains Rivera, knowledge means "an attempt to grasp, to comprehend, to gain control over people," and was used as "a key strategy of colonial domination."[16] The mission strategy based on that knowledge implies an "intricate relation between colonial strategies of objectification and control over others, and an objectifying vision of God."[17] Even now, Evangelical and neo-Calvinist churches continue such colonial missionary activities, consciously or unconsciously.[18]

In addition, the visual image of Jesus as racially white was used as a mission strategy. Portraits of the white Jesus suggested the superiority of whiteness and effectively supported colonial missionary efforts. As theologian and visual arts specialist Sheila Winborne illustrates in her essay, "Images of Jesus in Advancing the Great Commission,"[19] among the portraits of Jesus, the "Head of Christ," painted by commercial artist Warner Sallman, in which Jesus is depicted with blond hair and European features, was the most popular because of its massive commercial distribution.[20] As an expression of the European cultural perception of Jesus, this painted cultural image reinforced the white racial superiority created by European colonialists and churches when it was used for missionary purposes in the name of the Great Commission. Jesus as white represents the superiority of whites as God's chosen people and persons of color as an "Other,"[21] subjugated to servitude. The Christian mission, supported by such an artwork, spread notions of white superiority and led missionaries to treat the indigenous people of color disrespectfully as objects of their agenda rather than as sacred beings of dignity.[22]

A Postcolonial Intertextual Reading

While postcolonial and other liberation theologians have made efforts to disclose the imperial nature of the Great Commission and its destructive influence on the colonized, the task of preaching on the Great Commission requires more than criticism of the traditional interpretation and its negative impact on non-Europeans. The pressing concern for preaching from a postcolonial perspective is how to decolonize the text and reappropriate it to provide the churches with constructive theological guidance for their missions in the neo- and postcolonial world.

The Great Commission is a part of the canon of the Christian community, which should be used as the point of departure for reflection on the faith and life of the Christian church. The prerequisite when reading the Great Commission as a conversation starter should be to regard it as an "other," i.e., something written for different readers in different social locations.[23] Reading this text as "other" is like "a dialogue with a stranger,"[24] someone who lives in a culturally and socially different world. To have a conversation with the stranger, we need to enter that stranger's realm by seeing with their eyes. If we fail to encounter the biblical text as a stranger and ignore the distance between its sociocultural and historical context and our own, our reading risks using the Bible as a prooftext to validate our own prejudices and maintain the status quo.[25] The Western colonialist reading of the Great Commission is a stark example of this failure and ignorance.

When we read the Great Commission from a postcolonial perspective, the most critical problem becomes Matthew's expression of the charge in the imperative mood and the imperialist tone in verses 19–20a: "Go therefore and make disciples of all nations, baptizing them in the name of the Father and of the Son and of the Holy Spirit, and teaching them to obey everything that I have commanded you." In these verses, as colonialist readers understand them, the risen Jesus sounds like an authoritarian military commander deploying his army to conquer the whole world. However, postcolonial biblical scholar Warren Carter helps us read these verses in their particular historical and cultural context. According to Carter, the Gospel of Matthew was probably written in the 80s CE, in the city of Antioch in Syria. The audience was living "in the tough, rural-urban hierarchical environment" there as a small, marginalized group of the colonized, resisting "the values, commitments, and agendas of the Roman empire."[26] In this situation,

CHAPTER 5

Matthew writes his Gospel mimicking the colonizers' language and tone in a subtle way:

> It [the Gospel of Matthew] mirrors imperial realities, even while it contests them. It protests imperial power, even while it imitates imperial structures, language and ways of being. It advocates an alternative identity and way of life, even while recognizing a continuing accommodated existence. It envisages the future and violent triumph of God's power and empire over Rome (24.27–31), even while it forms a community that renounces violence (5.43–44) and structures that embody "power over" others. (20.25–26)[27]

When we read Matthew's Great Commission considering these tensions, we can recognize his engagement with the imperial culture through "imitation yet critique."[28] On the one hand, Matthew engages with the imperial culture by mimicking its way of being and linguistic expressions of the Roman imperial culture. On the other hand, he shapes "the Gospel's own imperial-imitating system of dominating power and sovereignty"[29] by commissioning the disciples to expand the reign of God, which is the alternative to the Roman imperial system. In other words, the Great Commission is a continuation of the Jesus Movement that resists the Roman Empire by expanding a new community through baptism in the name of the Triune God and Jesus' teaching. Hence, just as the Gospel of Matthew is "a product of imperial power and productive of its own imperial system of power,"[30] so too is the Great Commission. It best attests to this dual mode by imitating imperial language and hierarchical structures in the imperative mood and, at the same time, by advocating an alternative community of the baptized. At this point, Dube's criticism that the Great Commission is "an imperialist text . . . that articulates an ideology of imperialism"[31] is half right. She nevertheless overlooks "the ambiguities and complicities it attests to in negotiating its imperial context" that are implied in "hybridity, mimicry, assimilation,

[and] agency."³² Worse than that, the Western missionaries' literalistic interpretations of the Great Commission not only neglect Matthew's dual mode, but also distort the implied meaning of the Great Commission.

How then might the preacher bring up the forgotten or neglected parts of the text that are ambiguated by its imperialist mode and help listeners comprehend the implied meaning of the Great Commission? In answer to this question, Indian Jesuit priest and biblical scholar George M. Soares-Probhu interprets the Great Commission through a postcolonial intertextual reading.³³ Many Western biblical scholars use the term "intertextuality" to refer to a way of interpreting a biblical text by referencing other texts within the Bible, and the term "extratextuality" for referencing other sacred texts or religious traditions.³⁴ Yet postcolonial scholars do not limit the use of the term intertextuality to the Bible. They see it as a method of reading the biblical text in dialogue, not only with other biblical texts, but also with other communally inspired sacred texts and traditions.³⁵ In this sense, to use Kwok's term, intertextuality is a form of dialogical imagination.³⁶ By reading the biblical text along with other religious texts, a postcolonial intertextual reading rejects the exclusively Bible-centered Western biblical hermeneutics and seeks a truthful meaning of the text in the trust that the God who spoke through the Christian Scriptures has spoken through other sacred texts also, so that they might help draw out "the divine meaning latent in Scripture."³⁷

From the many methods of intertextual reading, such as allusion, echo, quotation, juxtaposition, typology, irony, Midrash, allegory, and metaphor, Soares-Probhu uses juxtaposition. He parallels the Great Commission and a Buddhist text about a "mission command" given by the Buddha to his first followers in the *Mahavagga*, a section of the *Vinaya* texts of the *Pali* Canon.³⁸ He compares the historical backgrounds and literary forms of these two texts and identifies their similarities and differences. According to his reading, some differences in the content of the two help us better understand the implicit meaning of the Great Commission, a meaning that has often been neglected by the Christian church. One difference is that while Matthew grounds the mission command solely in the authority of Jesus and imposes the duty of the mission on the disciples, the Buddhist mission command is grounded not only in the authority of the Buddha as the Enlightened ("I am delivered, O Bhikkus, from all fetters human and divine"), but also in the similar authority his disciples have achieved through their enlightenment ("You, O Bhikkus, are also delivered from all fetters, human and divine").[39]

Another difference between the two texts is that the Buddhist version clearly states the purposes of the mission while Matthew's text is not explicit about this. The Buddhist text says that the disciples are sent out "for profit of many, for the happiness of many, and out of compassion for the world."[40] It also mentions that the Buddha's disciples are qualified to fulfill these purposes by "proclaim[ing] a consummate, perfect and pure life of holiness,"[41] for they are the enlightened, as the Buddha is himself. By contrast, in Matthew's text, the purpose of the mission is missing. It mentions neither the welfare of "all nations" (v. 19a) to whom the disciples are being sent, nor the character of Jesus' disciples who will serve as missionaries. Instead, the nations seem to be treated as mere "objects of mission,"[42] and the disciples are sent regardless of their state of maturity. As a result, Soares-Prabhu concludes, the Western colonialist mission based on the Great Commission ceases to be an act of service and becomes "a sinful exercise of institutional survival, expansion, or power."[43]

The Buddhist intertext challenges us to ponder these two ambiguous dimensions of the Great Commission: the purpose of the Christian mission and the character of the disciples who are sent as missionaries. A solution to these problems can be found in rereading the Great Commission, especially verses 19 and 20a, through an intertextual approach within the Bible. Such a reading suggests that the Buddhist statement about the purposes of the mission ("all mission must be for the good, the profit, the happiness of the world and human beings")[44] and the description of the readiness of the missionaries as living Buddhas correspond to those of Christianity. In fact, Matthew's composition of the Great Commission is itself a product of an intertextual approach. Its literary genre is a farewell discourse with a commission prior to someone's departure as in Moses's farewell discourse in Deuteronomy 33. It includes the doubt motif (v. 17), alluding to Luke 24:11 in which the disciples do not believe the women's witnesses to the risen Jesus and the story of doubting Thomas in John 20:25. Furthermore, the command to baptize all nations (v. 19) is equivalent to the risen Jesus' command to remit sins found in Luke 24:47 and John 20:20–23. The declaration of the risen Jesus, "All authority in heaven and on earth has been given to me" (v. 18), echoes the Son of Man tradition in Daniel 7:14, while the promise of the abiding presence of the risen Jesus (v. 20) is associated with those in Luke 24:49 and John 20:22.[45]

An intertextual reading of verses 19 and 20a—in which the risen Jesus instructs his hearers to make disciples of all nations by baptizing and teaching them—provides us with some clarity about the purposes of the Christian mission and the character of the missionaries in relation to the theological meaning of baptism and teaching. Jesus' command to baptize in the Trinitarian formula (v. 19b) sounds somewhat abrupt, for Matthew does not explain why baptism is important in their mission. However, Paul the Apostle helps us understand the profound meaning of baptism as follows:

> As many of you as were baptized into Christ have clothed yourselves with Christ. There is no longer Jew or Greek, there is no longer slave or free, there is no longer male and female; for all of you are one in Christ Jesus. And if you belong to Christ, then

CHAPTER 5

you are Abraham's offspring, heirs according to the promise. (Gal. 3:27–29)

According to Paul, baptism creates a community based on egalitarian social relations. In the community of the baptized, people are treated equally in love and with respect as friends. Baptism is the rite of initiation to enter this community of friends. It is not coerced through force but is instead a response to the nudge of the Holy Spirit through choice. In this sense, the expansion of the community of the baptized that the risen Jesus commissions his disciples to carry out is an anti-imperial movement. While Roman rule is based on the hierarchical military power of violence, "[t]he basis of friendship is freedom," with the "commitment to the other, a commitment to stay true, and to stay trustworthy."[46] The purpose of the mission with which the risen Jesus commissions his disciples is, therefore, that of multiplying the community of friends who pursue the well-being and happiness of one another, just as it is with the Buddhist mission.

An intertextual reading of verse 20a, "and teaching them to obey everything that I have commanded you," implies the readiness of the disciples/missionaries. For Matthew, disciples are those who are called to follow Jesus and respond positively to his call by living their lives as he instructs them. What then are his instructions? They are explicit in chapters 5 to 7, 10, 13, 18, and 24 to 25. In these chapters, he teaches the disciples about a new identity and the new communal lifestyle appropriate to that new identity: forgiving the sins of their enemies and praying for those who persecute them, rather than striking back. In doing so, their enemies become their friends.[47] Jesus gives these teachings, not only in words, but also by demonstrating them through his ministry to the point of death on the cross. Here it is noteworthy that the word "teach" in Old English is *tæcan*, which means "to show" or "to demonstrate."[48] The disciple who is enlightened by Jesus, the Enlightened One, is to live their life as an "infectious witness of a genuine Christian life,"[49] or as a living Jesus, or as "light" and "salt" (Matt. 5:13–16). This is the character of the disciples who are sent out to all nations as missionaries. By living such a life, they can show what Jesus taught them: to love one another as friends.

The intertextual reading of verses 19 and 20a deepens our understanding of the Great Commission in connection with John 15:12–17:

> This is my commandment, that you love one another as I have loved you. No one has greater love than this, to lay down one's life for one's friends. You are my friends if you do what I command you. I do not call you servants any longer, because the servant does not know what the master is doing; but I have called you friends, because I have made known to you everything that I have heard from my Father. You did not choose me but I chose you. And I appointed you to go and bear fruit, fruit that will last, so that the Father will give you whatever you ask in my name. I am giving you these commands so that you may love one another.

This passage alludes to the notion that the disciples/missionaries are those who are appointed by Jesus to "go and bear fruit" by making friends with those in all nations (not only Jews but also gentiles), through love, and to the point of laying down their lives for them as Jesus did. More directly, the Christian mission is to build friendship with the other, making friends with those who are on the margins of society.

The intertextual reading of the Great Commission thus interprets it as the *missio Dei* (the mission of God)—of building "a viable koinonia or community of friends,"[50] in which all enjoy "supreme welfare."[51] It is a Christian calling to friendship with the other, as God in Jesus is in friendship with us. It is an invitation to communion—a community of friends—following the lead of the Holy Spirit. This interpretation is strikingly different from that of the Western colonialist, which is based on the ideology of white supremacy and has often led the Christian mission to be "more preoccupied with aggrandizement of the missioner rather than the welfare of the missionized."[52]

Jesus as Postcolonial Friend

Whereas the tone of the Great Commission gives the impression that the risen Jesus is a commander or an authoritarian teacher who orders his disciples on an urgent task of the mission, the postcolonial intertextual reading of the text helps us arrive at a more rounded interpretation, in which Jesus is recognized as a friend and the Great Commission as an invitation to friendship. Generally, a friend is a person who is in a mutual relationship with a commitment to common values and interests. As theologian Dana Robert succinctly summarizes, the common classical concept of friendship among Chinese sages, such as Confucius, and Greek and Latin philosophers, such as Aristotle and Cicero, represents this understanding of a friend. For these, friendship is a mutual relationship between two males who are equal in status, ability, and age, standing side by side like brothers. That means friendship belongs to "privileged male elites."[53] As "an incubator of aristocratic male values," friendship "is shared rather than one-sided, and it encourages virtue that improves the individual person and undergirds an orderly society."[54] In contemporary Western culture, which is dominated by excessive individualism, neoliberal capitalism, and the sort of mobility that nurtures contractual or competitive relationships, friends are often regarded as people we can retreat to in our private relations, and friendship tends to "superficial attachments" or "a private relationship and a play form of sociability,"[55] as practical theologian Anne-Marie Ellithorpe points out.

Yet the postcolonial intertextual reading helps us understand that Jesus' identity as a friend and his friendship are different from those of the worldwide classical or Western individualistic conceptions. Instead, his identity as a postcolonial friend and his postcolonial friendship are based on four distinctive characteristics. First, the image of Jesus as a postcolonial friend reflects the very nature of God depicted in the relational understanding of the Trinity. The Trinity means the communion of three Persons in which each one flourishes through the love of the others, and the essence of this Trinitarian relationship is the model of friendship.[56] Jesus' friendship with others illustrates the Trinitarian divine friendship, which is "loving one another in ways that appreciate both otherness and intimacy and that affirm and celebrate differences."[57] The friendship of the Trinity helps us interpret the *imago Dei* motif in the creation narrative in Genesis in this way: "[F]riendship is 'God's image in humankind,'" and human beings are image-bearers of the Triune God as friendship.[58] Jesus as a postcolonial friend invites human beings into this friendship of the Trinity, this *koinonia*, or communion. The Trinitarian formula of baptism in Matthew 28:19b connotes that baptism is the initiation rite for entering into the community of friendship with the Triune God.

The second characteristic of Jesus' friendship is inclusivity. Unlike the exclusive classical concept of friendship, Jesus' friendship is open, not limited to the inner circle of his equals, but inclusive of others of different status. He is a friend, not only of his first disciples, but also of those beyond the boundaries of ethnicity, gender, and class. He lived his life as a friend of both colonized and colonizers. He shared the suffering and pain of the colonized and loved them to the point of his death in solidarity with them. At the same time, he made friends with colonizers by forgiving their sins and transforming them from the agents of the Roman Empire into agents of the reign of God. As a postcolonial friend, Jesus invites his disciples to befriend these others in "all nations" crossing cultural, geographical, social, gender, and class boundaries. This "boundary-crossing friendship" of Jesus[59] represents the essence of postcolonial missions.

The third characteristic of Jesus' postcolonial friendship is that it is communal, not private. He makes friends with those who are not his equals, and his friendship with them empowers their communities to be transformed into communities of friends. His communal social friendship is epitomized in his shared meals with outcasts and strangers and the denunciation he received as "a friend of tax collectors and sinners" (Matt. 11:19; Luke 7:34). His friendship with these people fosters a commitment to care, justice, and love, and challenges them to live out their friendship with Jesus in their own communities by befriending and helping the poor and the needy. Acts 2:42–47 exemplifies the new lifestyle of the community of friends who share their possessions, as well as the apostles' teaching and fellowship, the breaking of bread, and the prayers. This community of friends, which was a powerful counter model to the imperial society of the Roman Empire, is the prototype of postcolonial friendship. It is not an exclusive private relationship or "a play form of sociability,"[60] unconcerned and uninvolved in public matters, but "social friendship" concerned with "how we live together in community,"[61] and a "solidarity friendship"[62] of caring for one another by becoming companions, advocates, and partners.

These three characteristics of Jesus' friendship culminates in the last characteristic of postcolonial friendship, which is a cross-cultural relationship. This is a biblical practice, for we remember that Jesus made friends across ethnic, religious, cultural, and gender boundaries during his ministry.[63] The last words of Jesus on earth, according to Matthew, are also about this cross-cultural friendship. The risen Jesus commissions his disciples to continue building this cross-cultural friendship to the end of the age (Matthew 28:19–20). Cross-cultural friendship is essential for the Christian mission in our pluralistic postcolonial world, because it is crucial for building a global community that pursues racial and religious harmony among peoples of different faiths and cultures. By making friends with others cross-culturally, we recognize the deadly consequences of colonial and neocolonial systems that have victimized the powerless geopolitically, and we can have a clearer picture of living solidarity with them toward the reign of God, i.e., "shalom—the vision of peace, salvation, and justice about which Jesus spoke."[64]

Preaching Jesus as a postcolonial friend means building an inclusive, social, and cross-cultural friendship that imitates the divine friendship. It is missional preaching with a global responsibility for enhancing the welfare of all human life. By proclaiming Jesus as a symbol of postcolonial friendship, preachers can invite listeners to participate in building this global community of friends. Just as the Great Commission is about neither the conversion of listeners from their indigenous religions into Christianity, nor the "inculcation of Christian ideas into gentile minds,"[65] missional preaching does not aim at conversion, even if such a thing happens as a byproduct. Instead, preachers approach "the other," not "as an object of conversion" but as "an equal subject,"[66] and help their listeners experience "Transformation—metamorphosis"[67] by guiding them to enter a new dimension of their own faith traditions. In doing so, they might become agents who renew their own faith communities to participate in promoting justice and peace in our pluralistic postcolonial world. More precisely, as Paul's conversion story (Acts 9:1–30) and the Cornelius-Peter episode (Acts 10) illustrate, missional preaching is to help listeners become rooted in their faith traditions, while learning more about the forgotten aspects of those traditions, so as to renew their minds about becoming friends with others who are culturally and religiously different.

To achieve these purposes of missional preaching, preachers need a cosmopolitan identity of "cultural intelligence" and "cultural competence,"[68] through which they can embody divine friendship by honoring the full humanity of "the other" as a fellow friend of God. This requires of preachers' humility and respect for other cultures and religious traditions. If they are citizens of the

American Empire and have enjoyed the benefits of colonialism and neocolonialism intergenerationally, self-emptying becomes another step toward meeting the standards for preaching Jesus as a postcolonial friend. Such qualifications can never be fully obtained; they require lifelong discipline.

Missional preaching, or preaching Jesus as a postcolonial friend, is a way of participating in the creation of the worldwide "beloved community," where postcolonial friendship is practiced as a sign pointing to the possibility of reconciliation between colonizers and colonized. In this sense, all preaching should be missional. It is a call for "a worldwide fellowship," as Martin Luther King, Jr. articulates it, "a call for an all-embracing and unconditional love for all men [sic]."[69] With its potential to offer alternative perceptions of reality, Christian preaching can help listeners renew their personal and communal identities in the light of God's freedom and concern for the welfare of "all nations."

HOMILETICAL STRATEGIES: META PREACHING

Preaching Jesus as a postcolonial friend challenges preachers to reflect critically on who our friends are, and to think creatively about how preaching can contribute to building friendship with the other in the pluralistic postcolonial world. The global surge of migrants from former colonized countries to the metropoles has shifted racial and ethnic demographics around the globe. The United States, like other Western colonial and neocolonial countries, is not monocultural or monoracial. We witness economic disparities, cultural imperialism, white supremacy, and racism in our daily lives, locally as well as globally, because of colonialism and neocolonialism, and wonder how we preachers can help people discern "the will of God—what is good and acceptable and perfect" (Rom. 12:2)—around these social issues and with that understanding, how we can build a community of friends. Indeed, the primary locus of the Great Commission is our "glocal" community, that is, a community reflecting the convergence of both global and local concerns.

How then can we preach Jesus as a postcolonial friend in a global context? One idea may be that we practice "meta preaching," a self-reflective and questioning approach to the methods, procedures, and assumptions traditionally applied to homiletics. *Meta* is from the Greek, meaning "beyond," "after," or "behind." According to the Merriam-Webster Dictionary, *meta* is "usually used with the name of a discipline to designate a new but related discipline designed to deal critically with the original one."[70] The self-reflective nature of *meta* suggests that meta preaching goes beyond the conventional practice of preaching by expanding its horizons and using nontraditional homiletical strategies.

Meta preaching regards real life situations as the loci for preaching, rather than limiting a sermonic message to the sanctuary pulpit and regular worship times. In this broad understanding, meta preaching includes not only public discourse from a pulpit, but also any personal or private dialogue with the other. Wherever we meet "the other"—grocery stores, parks, coffee shops, restaurants, workplaces, airplanes, train stations, community potluck gatherings, town hall meetings, children's soccer fields, hospital waiting rooms, nursing home lobbies, etc.—can be considered places for preaching or for building a postcolonial friendship. Every encounter with the stranger can be a moment of preaching Jesus as a postcolonial friend and extending the divine friendship.

This idea reminds us of the significance of personal conversation in preaching. Personal conversation is an effective communication tool for creating a rapport or a friendly, harmonious relationship with others in both private and public arenas. It is notable that Buddhism and Confucianism also regard personal and private dialogue as the most effective tool of religious discourse. Both religions hold that truth is revealed through conversation between master and disciple or between masters, rather than through oratorical public speech, and that conversation partners are enlightened through insightful words and even "cryptic riddles" (a *koan* in Japanese or *hwadu* in Korean).[71]

By attending to the pain of people who come from the other parts of the globe, whether at one time or currently colonized, we can listen to them without becoming defensive. And by sharing problems, joys, and testimonies in times of predicament or celebration, we can experience a moment in the presence of the risen Jesus, as a friend with and among them. There are numerous examples of a personal conversation in the Bible that can be considered meta preaching. One of these is the profound theological conversation between Jesus and the Samaritan woman in John 4:4–42. Their personal conversation is an event of meta preaching in the sense that both make friends beyond their ethnic, gender, and religious differences through a private and intimate dialogue that ultimately transforms not only the woman but also her community.[72] Another example of meta preaching is the story of Zacchaeus in Luke 19:1–10. The conversation with Jesus transforms Zacchaeus into a friend of Jesus and restores his friendship with his community. The personal conversation between the risen Jesus and the two disciples on the road to Emmaus and the subsequent supper together at Emmaus, narrated in Luke 24:13–35, and the conversation between the risen Jesus and the six disciples when breaking the bread and sharing fish by the Sea of Galilee, in John 21:1–14, also illustrate meta preaching. All these events happen through Jesus initiating conversations during visits to the places where people are.

Meta preaching as a personal conversation reminds us that the word "sermon" is rooted in the Latin *sermo*, meaning private conversation. The term homily, which is from Greek *homilia*, also means an "informal, popular, familiarly conversational" style of preaching in a liturgical context.[73] Roman philosopher Cicero explains *vis ortionis* (the power of oratory) as consisting of two parts: argument (*contentio*) and *sermo* (conversation). While *contentio* is "ascribed to the debates in the courts and public assemblies, the senate," *sermo* is a manner of speech employed "in social circles, in philosophical debates, and in meetings of friends."[74] He further instructs on rhetoric for *sermo* as follows:

> The voice should be clear (*clara*) and pleasant (*suavis*) (1,133). Conversation (*sermo*) should be light (*lenis*), witty (*lepos*), and not obstinate (*minimeque pertinax*) . . . We ought to take the greatest care to show respect and have a special regard for those with whom we conduct our conversation (1.136). In conversation one should never be harsh or angry, though it may be necessary to appear angry sometimes.[75]

While these conversational skills are useful for meta preaching as a private conversation, they are also effective for meta preaching in a public place, since preaching as public discourse is not separate, but lies on a continuum from private to public. By using those conversational skills, preachers can avoid prescriptive and psychologically manipulative speech that dominates and cajoles listeners, and instead create a mood to build friendship. Therefore, meta preaching by means of the personal conversational style of communication makes it possible for preachers to preach Jesus as a postcolonial friend and to extend postcolonial friendship for the sake of social harmony and the welfare of all nations.

Sermon

A Letter to Mary and Elizabeth (Luke 1:39–45)[1]

I.

Our Gospel text is one of the most
beautiful stories in the Bible.
It is about Mary's visit to Elizabeth,
after Gabriel, the angel, announced
her unexpected pregnancy.
Perplexed
she visited her cousin-sister Elizabeth
as he told her to do.

. . . .

After reading their beautiful story,
I wrote them a letter
on behalf of us all,
gathered here in this place:

. . . .

Dear Mary and Elizabeth,
Greetings from the United States,
from a group of church leaders
on the other side of the planet
two-thousand years after you.

Sermon

For two millennia,
your stories have inspired countless people.
This evening, we also heard your story.
We were amazed by
your sisterhood in a time of crisis.
Both of you were pregnant, unusually so.

Mary,
a teenage girl, betrothed to Joseph,
pregnant without his involvement.

Elizabeth,
a senior citizen,
too old for childbirth,
probably menopausal.
Yet you too miraculously pregnant!
Luke calls your pregnancies as joyful events,
God's intervention announced by angels.
Yet how complicated it all must have been.

Mary,
your out-of-wedlock pregnancy
must have been big trouble,
though we do not know the full story:
How could your fiancé, family, and
neighbors understand.
You could have been disgraced,
stoned even.
How sacred you might have been as you began to show!
But, instead, you left the cove of fear and anxiety,
and ran to your cousin-sister Elizabeth,
who welcomed you in the Spirit!

Elizabeth,
how excited you must have been

Sermon

to learn you were with child.
In a society where
a woman had a duty
to bear a son for the family line,
you could not fulfill this duty and
had to live as a "sinner,"
in the eyes of your patriarchal society.
But you endured suffering by living in the Spirit.

Elizabeth,
How hard your pregnancy might have been,
bearing a child at such an age.
Your body might have been too weak
to hold the little one inside.

Mary,
God blessed you with Elizabeth,
who helped you see God's will,
God's wonderful plan for you and your son,
in your hour of confusion.

Elizabeth,
the Spirit in you was so contagious
it moved into Mary and
empowered her to imagine a new world
and become a prophet,
singing aloud a new song—
praising God's mercy,
prophesying God's judgment on the
proud, the mighty, and the rich,
and proclaiming God's blessing on
the lowly and the hungry.

[The congregation stands and sings "The Magnificat"[2]]

Sermon

Refrain-all: My soul proclaims your greatness, O Lord;

I sing my Savior's praise!
Great wonders you have done for me,
And holy is your name.
Verse 1: My soul proclaims your greatness, Lord;
I sing my Savior's praise!
Now every land and every age this blessing shall proclaim—
great wonders you have done for me, and holy is your name.
Refrain-all
Verse 2: To all who live in holy fear
your mercy ever flows.
With mighty arm you dash the proud,
their scheming hearts expose.
The ruthless you have cast aside, the lowly throned instead;
The hungry filled with all good things, the rich sent off unfed.
Refrain-all
Verse 3: To Israel, your servant blest,
your help is ever sure;
The promise to our parents made their children will secure.
Sing glory to the Holy One, give honor to the world,
And praise the Power of the Most
High, one God, by all adored.
Refrain-all

. . . .

Mary,
how radical and revolutionary your song
banned through human history
from public singing—
banned by the British colonial authorities in India
in the 1800s,
banned by the ruling military junta
in Argentina in the 1970s

Sermon

after the "Mothers of the Disappeared" made it
a song of nonviolent resistance,
and banned by the military regime
of Guatemala in 1980s.[3]
The new world you imagined was a threat to them all.

Mary and Elizabeth,
how radical and revolutionary you were!
With the new world you imagined,
the new world you eagerly anticipated
for you and your children yet to be born,
generation after generation.

II.

Mary and Elizabeth,
our world is so very different from yours
in democracy, equality, and the status of women,
socially and professionally.
American women are no longer the servants of men,
and childbearing is just one path of many.
If you came back today,
You'd find women at the top,
Almost everywhere:
On the congressional floor,
in professional chairs,
on benches of judgment,
and behind the pulpit.
Our society is affluent also,
not poor or lowly as you were.
We are like a new Roman Empire,
living like Romans.
Slavery, exploitation, and the appropriation of resources
from Africa, Asia, and Latin America.
That is the backbone of

our nation's wealth,
the benefit of colonialism.
Our economy and military make us proud and mighty,
on the thrones of judgment of a world
that belongs to God.
We are in no great position
to sing your song with joy.
We dare not praise the God
who favors your own—
the colonized, the poor, and the lowly.

III.

But we must admit
our world is not so very far from yours.
So many stricken in poverty,
victims of colonialism, capitalism, and individualism,
our endless pandemics of supremacism,
sexism, and racism,
regional and national wars,
the invasion of imperialism,
millions of innocent homeless
seeking refuge and shelter,
sexual harassment and violence with guns
in home, workplace, school, and church.
Moreover,
animals, plants, waters, and soils
suffer destruction at our hands.
Although we should treat God's creation with respect,
as our Native American friends remind us,
we exploited it
for our "enrichment, enjoyment and comfort,"
doing critical damage.[4]
We know
our world cannot continue like this.

SERMON

We know
we cannot bequeath it like this
to our children, grandchildren, great-
grandchildren, and beyond.

IV.

Mary and Elizabeth,
the children in your wombs were blessed
because you imagined a different world,
and raised them with this vision.
No wonder John became the forerunner of the Messiah
and Jesus "the image of the invisible
God" (Colossians 1:15).

Sister Elizabeth,
Transmit the Holy Spirit to us
so that we may see the world through God's eyes,
not only for us
but also for our children yet to be born,
a world where the proud are scattered,
the lowly are lifted up,
the hungry are fed,
and the rich are sent empty away.
Whoever we are,
and whatever we do,
we need the life-giving Spirit
with the power to
renew our calling and
change our thinking and living
so that together we might generate life,
the life of all living creatures on the earth.

Sister Mary,
sing your song for us again and again

Sermon

so that we may learn to sing along
with our churches, neighbors, and the world,
not only in words but also in deeds.
Sister Mary and Sister Elizabeth,
Bless us with imagination to
live as faithful disciples of God
in our time of crisis,
as fearlessly and compassionately as you did.

In Solidarity,
The conferees at the 2022 St. Olaf Conference

Notes

Preface

1. Sarah Travis, *Decolonizing Preaching: The Pulpit as Postcolonial Space* (Eugene, OR: Cascade Books, 2014); HyeRan Kim-Cragg, *Postcolonial Preaching: Creating a Ripple Effect* (Lanham, MD: Lexington Books, 2022). In addition, *Unmasking White Preaching: Racial Hegemony, Resistance, and Possibilities in Homiletics* (Lanham, MD: Lexington Books, 2022), ed. Andrew Wymer and Lis Valle-Ruiz, is a helpful resource.

2. Eunjoo M. Kim, *Preaching the Presence of God: A Homiletic from an Asian American Perspective* (Valley Forge, PA: Judson Press, 1999).

3. Letty Russell, *Just Hospitality: God's Welcome in a World of Difference* (Louisville, KY: Westminster John Knox Press, 2009).

4. Kim, *Preaching in an Age of Globalization* (Louisville, KY: Westminster John Knox Press, 2010); *Christian Preaching and Worship in Multicultural Contexts* (Collegeville, MN: Liturgical Press, 2017).

5. Kim, *Women Preaching: Theology and Practice through the Ages* (Cleveland, OH: Pilgrim Press, 2004).

6. Joyce Ann Mercer, "Feminist and Womanist Practical Theology," in *Opening the Field of Practical Theology: An Introduction*, ed. Kathleen A. Cahalan and Gordon S. Mikoski (Lanham, MD: Roman & Littlefield, 2014), 99–100.

Chapter 1

1. David G. Buttrick, *Preaching Jesus Christ: An Exercise in Homiletic Theology* (Philadelphia, PA: Fortress Press, 1988); Charles Campbell, *Preaching Jesus: New Directions for Homiletics in Hans Frei's Postliberal Theology* (Grand Rapids, MI: William B. Eerdmans Publishing Company, 1996); David Lose, *Preaching Jesus: Preaching in a Postmodern World* (Grand Rapids, MI: William B. Eerdmans Publishing Company, 2003); Annette Brownlee, *Preaching Jesus Christ Today: Six Questions for Moving from Scripture to Sermon* (Grand Rapids, MI: Baker Academic, 2018).

Notes

2. Ansel Min, *The Solidarity of Others in a Divided World: A Postmodern Theology after Postmodernism* (New York: T & T Clark International, 2004), 1.

3. Kwok Pui-lan, *Postcolonial Imagination and Feminist Theology*, (Louisville, KY: Westminster John Knox Press, 2005), 2–3.

4. J. Jorge Klor de Alva, "The Postcolonialization of the (Latin) American Experiences: A Reconsideration of 'Colonialism,' 'Postcolonialism,' and 'Mestizaje,'" in *After Colonialism: Imperial Histories and Postcolonial Displacements*, ed. Gyan Prakash (Princeton, NJ: Princeton University Press, 1995), 245.

5. Catherine Keller, *God and Power: Counter-Apocalyptic Journeys* (Minneapolis, MI: Augsburg Fortress Press, 2005), 99.

6. Kwok, *Postcolonial Imagination and Feminist Theology*, 127.

7. Letty Russell, *Just Hospitality*, 25.

8. Ibid., 26.

9. Andrew Wymer, "Betraying White Preaching: 'Responsible' and 'Realistic' White Preaching" (paper presented at the annual meeting of the Academy of Homiletics, Princeton, NJ, December 2019), 257 (https://d2r0txsugik6oi.cloudfront.net/neon/resource/academyofhomiletics/files/2019%20AOH%20Workgroup%20Papers%20Final.pdf).

10. Augustine, *On Christian Doctrine*, trans. D. W. Robertson, Jr. (New York: MacMillan Publishing Company), ix.

11. Sarah Travis, *Decolonizing Preaching: The Pulpit as Postcolonial Space*.

12. Ibid., 89.

13. Ibid., 125.

14. Ibid., 47.

15. The conference papers were published as an edited book by Andrew Wymer and Lis Valle-Ruiz, *Unmasking White Preaching*.

16. HyeRan Kim-Cragg, *Postcolonial Preaching*.

17. Catherine Keller, Michael Nausner, and Mayra Rivera, eds., *Postcolonial Theologies: Divinity and Empire* (St. Louis, MO: Chalice Press, 2004), 13.

18. Ibid., 55.

19. Homi Bhabha, *The Location of Culture*, 2nd ed. (Milton Park, UK: Routledge, 2004), 54.

20. Edward Said, "Secular Interpretation, the Geographical Element, and the Methodology of Imperialism," in *After Colonialism: Imperial Histories and Postcolonial Displacement*, ed. Gyan Prakash (Princeton, NJ: Princeton University Press, 1994), 36.

21. Said, *Culture and Imperialism* (New York: Vintage Books, 1994), 336.

22. Bhabha, *The Location of Culture*, 55.

23. Bhabha, *The Location of Culture*, 56.

24. Bhabha, "Culture's In-Between," in *Questions of Cultural Identity*, ed. Stuart Hall and Paul de Gay (New York: Sage Publications, 1996), 56.

25. Keller et al., eds., *Postcolonial Theologies*, 9.

NOTES

26. Tom Beaudoin, "Postmodern Practical Theology," in *Opening the Field of Practical Theology*, 190.
27. Tom Beaudoin, "Postmodern Practical Theology," 190.
28. Paul Ricoeur, *Oneself as Another*, trans. Kathleen Blamey (Chicago, IL: The University of Chicago Press, 1992); cf., Ricoeur, *The Course of Recognition*, tr. David Pellauer (Cambridge, MA: Harvard University Press, 2005).
29. Ibid., 19.
30. Ibid., 3.
31. Ibid., 18.
32. Ibid., 21.
33. Ibid., 318.
34. Thomas Talley, *The Origins of the Liturgical Year*, 2nd ed. (Collegeville, MN: Liturgical Press, 1991), 168–70.
35. According to Herman Wegman, in the time of Gregory the Great (590–604), the beginning of Lent was moved from Monday to the previous Wednesday, and later it was called Ash Wednesday. (Wegman, *Christian Worship in East and West: A Study Guide to Liturgical History*, tr. Gordon W. Lathrop (Collegeville, MN: Liturgical Press, 1985), 102.
36. Carol A. Newsom, Sharon H. Ringe, and Jacqueline E. Lapsley, eds., *Women's Bible Commentary*, 3rd ed. (Louisville, KY: Westminster John Knox Press, 2012), 716.
37. Musa W. Dube, "Reading for Decolonization (John 4.1–42)," in *John and Postcolonialism: Travel, Space, and Power*, ed. Musa W. Dube and Jeffrey L. Stanley (London: Sheffield Academic Press, 2002), 63.
38. Ibid., 67.
39. Mositi Torontle, *The Victims* (Gaborone: Botsalo, 1993), 57–58, quoted in Dube, "Reading for Decolonization (John 4.1–42)," 72–74.
40. Dube, "Reading for Decolonization (John 4.1–42)," 74.
41. Ibid., 75.
42. Sang Hyun Lee, *From a Liminal Place: An Asian American Theology* (Minneapolis, MN: Fortress Press, 2010), 22.
43. For a more detailed description of Asian American women's experiences, see my essay, "Preaching in the Asian American Feminist Theological Family," in *Preaching the Manifold Grace of God: Theologies of Preaching in the Early Twenty-First Century*, ed. Ronald J. Allen (Eugene, OR: Cascade Books, 2022), 208–9.
44. Warren Carter, *John and Empire: Initial Explorations* (New York: T & T Clark, 2008), 189–91.
45. Said, *Culture and Imperialism*, 318.
46. Ibid., 318.
47. Cf., Choi Hee An, *A Postcolonial Self: Korean Immigrant Theology and Church* (New York: SUNY Press, 2015).

48. Stephen Crites, "Narrative Quality of Experience," *Journal of the American Academy of Religion* 39, no. 3 (1971): 299.

CHAPTER 2

1. Aristotle, *Nicomachean Ethics*, Book VI: Chapter 5, Paragraph 5, in *The Basic Works of Aristotle*, ed. Richard McKeon (New York: Random House, 1941), 1027.

2. Alasdair MacIntyre, *After Virtue*, 2nd ed. (Notre Dame, IN: University of Notre Dame Press, 1984), 161–62; cf., Don S. Browning, *A Fundamental Practical Theology: Descriptive and Strategic Proposals* (Minneapolis, MN: Fortress Press, 1991), 2.

3. Richard Osmer, *Practical Theology: An Introduction* (Grand Rapids, MI: William B. Eerdmans Publishing Company, 2008), 84.

4. Mark Johnson, *The Body in the Mind: The Bodily Basis of Meaning, Imagination, and Reason* (Chicago: University of Chicago Press, 1987), 140.

5. Patrick Sherry, *Spirit and Beauty: An Introduction to Theological Aesthetics*, 2nd ed. (London: SCM Press, 2002), 111.

6. Cf., Corrine Ware, *Discover Your Spiritual Type: A Guide to Individual and Congregational Growth* (Lanham, MD: Rowman & Littlefield, 1995).

7. Karen Bray, "Ungrounded Innocence: Confronting Christian Culpability in White Nationalism," in *Doing Theology in the Age of Trump: A Critical Report on Christian Nationalism*, ed. Jeffrey W. Robbins and Clayton Crockett (Eugene, OR: Wipf and Stock Publishers, 2018), 46–47.

8. Ibid., 52.

9. Willie James Jennings, *The Christian Imagination: Theology and the Origins of Race* (New Haven, CN: Yale University Press, 2010), 6.

10. Kwok, *Postcolonial Imagination and Feminist Theology*, 29–51.

11. Ibid., 31–38.

12. Ibid., 42.

13. Ibid., 171.

14. Ibid., 174–82.

15. Ibid., 48–51.

16. Charles Campbell, *Preaching Jesus: The New Directions for Homiletics in Hans Frei's Postliberal Theology* (Grand Rapids, MI: Wm. B. Eerdmans Publishing, 1997), 189.

17. Ibid, 192–93.

18. Ibid., 77.

19. Ibid, 192.

20. Ibid., 197.

21. Ibid., 203.

22. Kathryn Tanner, *Theories of Culture: A New Agenda for Theology* (Minneapolis, MN: Fortress Press, 1997), 106.

23. Kwok, *Postcolonial Imagination and Feminist Theology*, 200.

24. Cf., James E. Loder and W. Jim Neidhardt, *The Knight's Move: The Relational Logic of the Spirit in Theology and Science* (Colorado Springs, CO: Holmers & Howard Publishers, 1992), 55–58.

25. Kathleen A. Cahalan, "Unknowing: Spiritual Practices and the Search for a Wisdom Epistemology," in *Christian Practical Wisdom: What it Is, Why It Matters*, Dorothy C. Bass, Kathleen A. Cahalan, Bonnie J. Miller-McLemore, James R. Nieman, Christian B. Scharen (Grand Rapids, MI: William B. Eerdmans Publishing Company, 2016), 277.

26. Henry Ward Beecher defines imagination as "the God-power in the Soul" in his *Yale Lectures on Preaching* (New York: J. B. Ford and Company, 1873), 110–11.

27. Paul Scott Wilson also says, "Imagination is inspired by faith and faith is strengthened by imagination," in *Imagination of the Heart: New Understandings in Preaching* (Nashville, TN: Abingdon Press, 1988), 17.

28. Quoted in Timothy Jones, "Black Preaching in Brown Places: Towards the Development of a Black Mestizo Homiletic," *Homiletic* 40, no. 1 (2015): 44.

29. Bhabha, *The Location of Culture*, 1.

30. For example, *The Revised Common Lectionary* includes it for the Third and Fourth Sundays of Advent in Years A, B, C. Wilda Gafney's *A Women's Lectionary for the Whole Church: A Multi-Gospel Single-Year Lectionary* also includes it for the first three Advent Sundays (New York: Church Publishing Incorporated, 2021), 2–3, 6, 8–9, 94–95, 262–63.

31. Gafney, A *Women's Lectionary for the Whole Church*, 261.

32. Osmer, *Practical Theology*, 1–30.

33. Jane Schaberg, *The Illegitimacy of Jesus: A Feminist Theological Interpretation of the Infancy Narratives* (New York: HarperCollins, 1987).

34. Elizabeth Johnson, *Truly Our Sister: A Theology of Mary in the Communion of Saints* (New York: Continuum, 2003), 152–53.

35. Luke 1:50–53 in *The People's Companion to the Breviary: The Liturgy of the Hours with Inclusive Language* (Indianapolis, IN: Carmelites of Indianapolis, 1997), printed on the inside back cover.

36. Elizabeth Johnson, "Mary, Mary, Quite Contrary," https://uscatholic.org/articles/201101/mary-mary-quite-contrary/ (September 15, 2022). The author says that this article was published in *U.S. Catholic Magazine* 68, no. 12 (December 2003): 12.

37. Walter Brueggemann, *Tenacious Solidarity: Biblical Provocations on Race, Religion, Climate, and the Economy*, ed. Davis Hankins (Minneapolis, MN: Fortress Press, 2018), 53.

38. Tink Tinker, "Relationship, Not Ownership: Indigenous Lands and Colonial Occupation," unpublished, p. 3. The author said this paper was originally published in *The Journal of Tribal Studies*, in Jorhat, India (January 2021).

39. Kyle Whyte, "Critical Investigations of Resilience: A Brief Introduction to Indigenous Environmental Studies and Sciences," *Daedalus: Journal of the American Academy of Arts and Sciences* 147, no. 2 (Spring 2018): 137.

40. Leanne Betasamosake Simpson, *As We Have Always Done: Indigenous Freedom Through Radical Resistance* (Minneapolis: University of Minnesota Press, 2020), 4.

41. Simpson, *As We Have Always Done*, 159.

42. Whyte, "Critical Investigations of Resilience," 138.

43. Isaiah 61:1–2; 42:7; 49:8–9; 58:6.

44. Cf., *The Revised Common Lectionary* includes Isaiah 61:1–4. 8–11 in the Third Sunday of Advent, Year B, with the Magnificat in Luke 1:46–55.

45. Cf., Johnson, "Mary, Mary, Quite Contrary," 12.

46. Miroslav Volf, *The End of Memory: Remembering Rightly in a Violent World* (Grand Rapids, MI: Wm. B. Eerdmans Publishing Company, 2006), 82.

47. Simpson, *As We Have Always Done*, 8.

48. Ibid., 101.

49. Ibid., 20.

50. Susan Connelly, "The Magnificat as Social Document," *Compass; Kensington* 48, no. 4 (Summer 2014): 8–11.

51. Simpson, *As We Have Always Done*, 184.

52. Joerg Rieger, *Theology in the Capitalocene: Ecology, Identity, Class, and Solidarity* (Minneapolis, MN: Fortress Press, 2022), 169–70.

53. Ibid., 175.

54. Cf., Ronald Allen, ed., *Patterns of Preaching: A Sermon Sampler* (St. Louis, MO: Chalice Press, 1998), 36.

55. See the sample sermon, "A Letter to Mary and Elizabeth," included at the end of this book.

56. Johnson, *Truly Our Sister*, 267.

CHAPTER 3

1. UNHCR, https://www.unrefugees.org/refugee-facts/ (August 18, 2022).

2. British Broadcasting Corporation, "How Many Ukrainian Refugees are There?" (August 18, 2022).

3. Jonathan Sacks, The Chief Rabbi's New Year Message BBC Online Religion & Ethics (2001), http://www.chiefrabbi.org/articles/other/rhbbc.htm (December 18, 2021).

4. Buttrick, *Preaching Jesus Christ*.

5. Cf., Robert H. Gundry, *Matthew: A Commentary on His Handbook for a Mixed Church under Persecution* (Grand Rapids, MI: William B. Eerdmans Publishing Company, 1982), 32–34.

6. Michael N. Jagessar and Stephen Burns, *Christian Worship: Postcolonial Perspectives* (Milton Park, UK: Routledge, 2014), 90, 98.

7. Chad Myers and Matthew Colwell, *Our God is Undocumented: Biblical Faith and Immigrant Justice* (Maryknoll, NY: Orbis Books, 2012), 168.

8. Said, "Secular Interpretation, the Geographical Element, and the Methodology of Imperialism," 37–38. Said calls this hermeneutical approach "contrapuntal reading" in *Culture and Imperialism*, 66.

9. Christie C. Neuger, "Pastoral Counseling as an Art of Personal Political Activism," in *The Arts of Ministry: Feminist-Womanist Approaches*, ed. Christie C. Neuger (Louisville, KY: Westminster John Knox Press, 1996), 110; Kathleen D. Billman and Daniel Migliore, *Rachel's Cry: Prayer of Lament and Rebirth of Hope* (Cleveland, OH: The Pilgrim Press, 1999), 99.

10. Carter, *Matthew and the Margins: A Sociopolitical and Religious Reading* (Maryknoll, NY: Orbis Books, 2000), 39.

11. Myers and Colwell, *Our God Is Undocumented*, 164.

12. In *Trauma and Grace: Theology in a Ruptured World* (Louisville, KY: Presbyterian Publishing Corp, 2009), 124–26, Serene Jones creates a story by imagining the two women, Mary the mother of Jesus, and a woman who loses her son in the massacre conducted by Herod. Her storyline presupposes that the death of the woman's baby is caused by the birth of Mary's son Jesus. However, the postcolonial approach retrieves the colonial condition of the historical context and understands that Matthew connects the colonial violence that his community experiences daily to the event of Jesus' birth to indict the cruelty of the colonial Roman Empire.

13. William Sloane Coffin, "The Task Ahead," in *Sanctuary: A Resource Guide for Understanding and Participating in the Central American Refugees' Struggle*, ed. Gary Maceoin (New York: HarperCollins, 1985), 179; Miguel de la Torre, *The U.S. Immigration Crisis: Toward an Ethics of Place* (Eugene, OR: Cascade Books, 2016), 12, 69.

14. Demetria Martinez, "Only Say the Word," in *Three Times a Woman*, ed. Alici Gaspar de Alba, Maria Herrera-Sobek, and Demetria Martinez (Tempe, AZ: Bilingual Review/Press, 1989), 145–56.

15. Chimayó is a village in New Mexico. Its natives are descendants of Spain's conquistadores during the sixteenth and seventeenth centuries.

16. Martinez, "Only Say the Word," 145–46.

17. Virgilio Elizondo, *Galilean Journey: The Mexican American Promise*, 2nd ed. (Maryknoll, NY: Orbis Books, 2005), 30.

18. Niambi Michele Carter, *American While Black: African Americans, Immigration, and the Limits of Citizenship* (Oxford, UK: Oxford University Press, 2019), 169.

19. Martinez, "Only Say the Word," 147–48.

20. Ariel Burger, *Witness: Lessons from Elie Wiesel's Classroom* (San Francisco, CA: HarperOne, 2019), 93.

21. Ibid., 93.

22. Zygmunt Bauman, *Liquid Times: Living in an Age of Uncertainty* (Cambridge, UK: Polity Publisher, 2006), 41.
23. Bauman, *Strangers at Our Door* (Cambridge, UK: Polity Publisher, 2016), 88.
24. Ricoeur, *Interpretation Theory: Discourse and the Surplus of Meaning* (Fort Worth: Texas Christian University Press, 1976), 87.
25. Paul Lehmann, *Ethics in a Christian Context* (San Francisco, CA: Harper San Francisco, 1976), 85.
26. Carter, *Matthew and the Margins*, 85.
27. Russell, *Just Hospitality*, 25–26.
28. Johann Baptist Metz, *Faith in History and Society: Toward a Practical Fundamental Theology* (Freiburg, Germany: Herder and Herder Publishing, 2007), 90.
29. Herbert Anderson and Edward Foley, *Mighty Stories, Dangerous Rituals: Weaving Together the Human and the Divine* (Hoboken, NJ: John Wiley and Sons, 1998), 170
30. Ibid., 168.
31. Ibid., 179.
32. Ibid.
33. Volf, *The End of Memory*, 82.
34. Brueggemann, *Tenacious Solidarity*, 250.
35. Russell, *Just Hospitality*, 82.
36. Ibid., 82.
37. De la Torre, "Why I'm Here," in *Preaching in/and the Borderlands*, ed. Dwayne Howell and Charles Aaron, Jr. (Eugene, OR: Pickwick Publications, 2020), 23.
38. Vincent de la Torre, "Trails of Hope and Terror," https://www.trailsofhopeandterrorthemovie.com/buy-the-film.html.
39. Shirley Murry and Carlton Young, "Star-Child" in *The Faith We Sing*, ed. Hoyt L. Hickman (Nashville, TN: Abingdon Press, 2000), #2095.

Chapter 4

1. Shelly Rambo, *Resurrecting Wounds: Living in the Afterlife of Trauma* (Waco, TX: Baylor University Press, 2017), 14.
2. John Calvin, *Commentary on the Gospel According to John*, vol. 2, tr. William Pringle (Grand Rapids, MI: Wm. B. Eerdmans Publishing Company, 1956), 2:250, quoted in Rambo, *Resurrecting Wounds*, 21).
3. Rambo, *Resurrecting Wounds*, 32.
4. Joseph Haroutunian, *Calvin: Commentaries* (London: SMC Press, 1958), 168, 240.
5. Rambo, *Resurrecting Wounds*, 21.
6. Haroutunian, *Calvin*, 169–70.
7. Ibid. 389.

NOTES

8. Rambo, *Resurrecting Wounds*, 20.
9. Ibid., 21.
10. Ibid.
11. Ibid., 27.
12. Ibid.
13. Williston Walker, Richard A. Norris, David W. Lotz, Robert T. Handy, *A History of the Christian Church*, 4th ed. (New York: Charles Scribner's Sons, 1985), 129.
14. It is ironic that Jesus was crucified because he designated himself as the Son of God, which was the title of the Roman emperors (John 19:7); Carter, *John and Empire*, 195.
15. Carter, *John and Empire*, 194–95.
16. Walker, et al., *A History of the Christian Church*, 152; Theological and Political Aspects of the Council of Chalcedon - DocsLib; Council of Chalcedon and Its Achievements | God and Man at Yale Divinity (garrettham.com) (April 15, 2023).
17. Rambo, *Resurrecting Wounds*, 27.
18. Saint Augustine, "Sermons on New Testament Lessons: Sermon LXIII," in *Nicene and Post-Nicene Fathers of the Christian Church*, Vol. VI, ed. Philip Schaff (Grand Rapid, MI: Wm. B. Eerdmans Publishing Company, 1979), 447–48.
19. Augustine, 326; cf., Andrew Sung Park, *Triune Atonement: Christ's Healing for Sinners, Victims, and the Whole Creation* (Louisville, KY: Westminster John Knox Press, 2009), 1–36.
20. Carter, *John and Empire*, 7.
21. Richard Horsley, *Jesus and Empire* (Minneapolis, MN: Augsburg Fortress Press, 2002), 28.
22. Allan Aubrey Boesak and Curtiss Paul DeYoung, *Radical Reconciliation: Beyond Political Pietism and Christian Quietism* (Maryknoll, NY: Orbis Books, 2018), 16–17.
23. Carter, *John and Empire*, 36.
24. Carter uses the method of "cultural intertextuality" as a basic hermeneutical tool throughout his entire book.
25. Carter, *John and Empire*, 37; cf., Barnabas Lindars, *The Gospel of John* (Grand Rapids, MI: Wm. B. Eerdmans Publishing Company, 1982), 29; F. F. Bruce, *The Gospel of John: Introduction, Exposition, and Notes*, reprint (Grand Rapids, MI: Wm. B. Eerdmans Publishing Company, 1984), 5, 11.
26. Ricoeur distinguishes between the immediate or primary memory and the secondary memory in *Memory, History, Forgetting*, tr. Kathleen Blamey and David Pellauer (Chicago: The University of Chicago Press, 2004), 32, 35.
27. Maurice Halbwachs, *On Collective Memory*, tr. Lewis A. Coser (Chicago: The University of Chicago Press, 1992), 199.
28. Carter, *John and Empire*, 14.

29. Cf., 19:15, "We have no king but Caesar."
30. Carter, *John and Empire*, 14.
31. Ibid., 5.
32. Ibid., 208.
33. Ibid., 215–16.
34. Ibid., 216.
35. Ibid.
36. Michel Foucault, "Nietzsche, Genealogy, History," in *The Foucault Reader*, ed. Paul Rabinow (New York: Pantheon Books, 1984), 93.
37. Ibid.," 93.
38. John McClure, *Other-wise Preaching: A Postmodern Ethic for Homiletics* (St. Louis, MO: Chalice Press, 2001), 42.
39. Ibid., 45.
40. Resmaa Menakem, *My Grandmother's Hands: Racialized Trauma and the Pathway to Mending Our Hearts and Bodies* (Las Vegas, NV: Central Recovery Press, 2017), xv–xvi.
41. Randy S. Woodly, *Indigenous Theology and the Western Worldview: A Decolonized Approach to Christian Doctrine* (Grand Rapids, MI: Baker Academic, 2022), 31–34.
42. William G. McLoughlin, *Champions of the Cherokees: Evan and John B. Jones* (Princeton, NJ: Princeton University Press, 1990), vi, quoted in Woodley, *Indigenous Theology and the Western Worldview*, 34–35.
43. Woodley, *Indigenous Theology and the Western Worldview*, 3.
44. Luke A. Powery, *Becoming Human: The Holy Spirit and the Rhetoric of Race* (Louisville, KY: Westminster John Knox Press, 2022), 21.
45. M. Shawn Copeland, *Enfleshing Freedom: Body, Race, and Being* (Minneapolis, MN: Fortress Press, 2010), 29, quoted in Powery, *Becoming Human*, 18.
46. Hortense J. Spillers, *Black, White and in Color: Essays on American Literature and Culture* (Chicago: The University of Chicago Press, 2003), 206–7.
47. Menakem, *My Grandmother's Hands*, 90.
48. Ibid., 73.
49. Ibid., 74.
50. Ibid., 75.
51. More accurately, "pervasive traumatic stress disorder" (Menakem, *My Grandmother's Hands*, footnote 8 on p. 15).
52. Menakem, *My Grandmother's Hands*, 15.
53. Boesak and DeYoung, *Radical Reconciliation*, 10.
54. Jennings, *The Christian Imagination*, 10.
55. Boesak and DeYoung, *Radical Reconciliation*, 12.
56. Ricoeur, *Memory, History, Forgetting*, 457, 464, 466, 467.
57. Ibid., 482.
58. Woodley, *Indigenous Theology and the Western Worldview*, x–xi, 52.
59. Boesak and DeYoung, *Radical Reconciliation*, 20.

60. Ibid., 20.
61. Ricoeur, *Memory, History, and Forgetting*, 494.
62. Travis, *Unspeakable: Preaching and Trauma-Informed Theology* (Eugene, OR: Cascade Books, 2021), 54.
63. David Augsburger, *Pastoral Counseling Across Cultures* (Philadelphia, PA: Westminster Press, 1986), 28.
64. Kim, *Preaching in an Age of Globalization*, 70.

Chapter 5

1. Dube, "'Go Therefore and Make Disciples of All Nations' (Matt 28:19a): A Postcolonial Perspective on Biblical Criticism and Pedagogy," in *Teaching the Bible: The Discourses and Politics of Biblical Pedagogy*, ed. Fernando F. Segovia and Mary Ann Tolbert (Maryknoll, NY: Orbis Books, 1998), 229.
2. Katie Cannon, "Christian Imperialism and the Transatlantic Slave Trade," *Journal of Feminist Studies in Religion* 24, no. 1 (2008); 127–34.
3. Steven T. Newcomb, *Pagans in the Promised Land: Decoding the Doctrine of Christian Discovery*, 3rd ed. (Chicago: Chicago Review Press—Fulcrum, 2008), 83.
4. Cannon, "Christian Imperialism and the Transatlantic Slave Trade," 127–28.
5. Ibid., 129.
6. Ibid., 131.
7. Ibid., 129.
8. Ibid., 130.
9. Ibid., 131.
10. Ibid., 133.
11. Notes of "Lecture on Missions" by Professor Dr. A. Kuyper, Given at the Mission Conference, Amsterdam, January 28–30, 1890, trs. Harry Van Dyke, 5–6, Kuyper on Missions (allofliferedeemed.co.uk (May 20, 2023).
12. Kuyper, "Lecture on Missions," 9.
13. Beatrice Okyere-Manu, "Colonial Mission and the Great Commission in Africa," in *Teaching All Nations: Interrogating the Matthean Great Commission*, ed. Mitzi J. Smith and Jayachitra Lalitha (Minneapolis, MN: Fortress Press, 2014), 24–25.
14. Ibid., 29.
15. Robert McLean, *Old Spain in New America* (New York: Association Press, 1916), 134, quoted in Mayra Rivera, *The Touch of Transcendence: A Postcolonial Theology of God* (Louisville, KY: Westminster John Knox Press, 2007), 10.
16. Rivera, *The Touch of Transcendence*, 10.
17. Ibid., 10.
18. Cf. Michale W. Goheen and Timothy M. Sheridan, *Becoming a Missionary Church: Lesslie Newbigin and Contemporary Church Movement* (Grand Rapids, MI: Baker Academic, 2022), 8–9.

19. Sheila Winborne, "Images of Jesus in Advancing the Great Commission," in *Teaching All Nations*, 159–74.
20. Winborne, "Images of Jesus in Advancing the Great Commission, 164–65.
21. Ibid., 165.
22. Woodley, *Indigenous Theology and the Western Worldview*, 45.
23. Kim, *Preaching in an Age of Globalization*, 67.
24. Ibid., 67.
25. Ibid., 67.
26. Carter, *Matthew and the Margins*, 2.
27. Carter, "The Gospel of Matthew," in *A Postcolonial Commentary on the New Testament Writings*, ed. Fernando F. Segovia and R. S. Sugirtharajah (New York: T & T Clark, 2009), 73.
28. Ibid., 72.
29. Ibid., 73.
30. Ibid.
31. Dube, "'Go Therefore and Make Disciples of All Nations' (Matt 28:19a)," 229.
32. Carter, "The Gospel of Matthew," 72.
33. George Soares-Probhu, "Two Mission Commands: An Interpretation of Matthew 28:16–20 in the Light of a Buddhist Text," in *Voices from the Margin: Interpreting the Bible in the Third World*, ed. R. S. Sugirtharajah, 2nd ed. (Maryknoll, NY: Orbis Books, 1997), 319–38.
34. Cf. Steve Moyise, "Intertextuality and the Study of the Old Testament in the New Testament," in *The Old Testament in the New Testament*, ed. Steve Moyise (London: Sheffield Academic Press, 2000), 14.
35. Sugiratharajah, *Asian Biblical Hermeneutics and Postcolonialism: Contesting the Interpretations* (Maryknoll, NY: Orbis Books, 1998), 23.
36. Kwok Pui-lan, *Postcolonial Imagination and Feminist Theology*, 38–44; see chapter 2 of this book.
37. Kim, *Christian Preaching and Worship in Multicultural Contexts* (Collegeville, MN: Liturgical Press, 2017), 53.
38. The *Pali* text: "At that time there were sixty-one Arahats [perfected persons] in the world; The Lord said to the Bhikkus [Buddhist monks], 'I am delivered, O Bhikkus, from all fetters human and divine; You, O Bhikkus, are also delivered from all fetters, human and divine; Go now, O Bhikkus, and wander for the profit of many, for the happiness of many, and out of compassion for the world, for the good, profit, and happiness of gods and human beings; let not two of you go the same way; Preach, O Bhikkus, the Dhamma, which is good in the beginning, good in the middle and good in the end in the spirit and in the letter. Proclaim a consummate, perfect and pure life of holiness . . . ; I will go also O Bhikkus, to Uruvela, to senanigama, in order to preach the dhamma." (Mahavagga, tr. T. W. Rhys Davids and Hermann Oldenberg, Published as Vinaya Texts, Part I in the Sacred Books of the East series vol. 13 (Varanasi,

Motilal Banarsidas, reprinted 1968), 112–13 in Soares-Prabhu, "Two Mission Commands," 327–28.

39. Soares-Prabhu, "Two Mission Commands," 331.
40. Ibid., 327.
41. Ibid., 328.
42. Ibid., 332.
43. Ibid.
44. Ibid.
45. James L. Mays, *Harper's Bible Commentary* (San Francisco, CA: Harper & Row Publishers, 1988), 981.
46. Sallie McFague, *Models of God: Theology for an Ecological, Nuclear Age* (Philadelphia, Pa.: Fortress Press, 1987), 162.
47. Cf. Chapter 4 of this book; Carter, "The Gospel of Matthew," 83.
48. Online Etymology Dictionary, sv. "teach," https://www.etymonline.com/word/teach#(23 June 2023).
49. Soares-Prabhu, "Two Mission Commands," 331.
50. Anne-Marie Ellithorpe, *Towards Friendship-Shaped Communities: A Practical Theology of Friendship* (Oxford, UK: Wiley Blackwell, 2022), 98.
51. Soares-Prabhu, "Two Mission Commands," 332.
52. IIbid. 333.
53. Dana Robert, *Faithful Friendships: Embracing Diversity in Christian Community* (Grand Rapids, MI: William B. Eerdmans Publishing Company, 2019), 32; cf. Ellithorpe, *Toward Friendship-Shaped Communities*, 109.
54. Ibid., 32.
55. Ellithorpe, *Toward Friendship-Shaped Communities*, 28.
56. Ibid., 141–44.
57. Ibid., 202.
58. Ibid., 78.
59. Robert, *Faithful Friendships*, 7.
60. Ibid., 28.
61. Ellithorpe, *Toward Friendship-Shaped Communities*, 27.
62. McFague, *Models of God*, 178.
63. Cf. John 4:5–30; Mark 7:24–30; Matthew 15:22; Matthew 8:5–13; Luke 7:10, etc.
64. Robert, *Faithful Friendships*, 166.
65. Sugirtharajah, "Interfaith Hermeneutics: An Example and Some Implications," in *Voices from the Margin*, 313.
66. Dube, "'Go Therefore and Make Disciples of All Nations' (Matt 28:19a)," 242.
67. Sugirtharajah, "Interfaith Hermeneutics," 311.
68. Robert, *Faithful Friendships*, 176.
69. Martin Luther King, Jr., *Where Do We Go from Here: Chaos or Community?* (Boston: Beacon Press, 1968), 201.

70. Merriam Webster, https://www.merriam-webster.com/dictionary/meta (May 21, 2023).
71. Kim, *Preaching the Presence of God*, 112.
72. See chapter 1 of this book.
73. William H. Willimon and Richard Lischer, *Concise Encyclopedia of Preaching* (Louisville, KY: Westminster/John Knox, 1995), 258.
74. Cicero, *De Officiis* 1.132, quoted in Robert W. Cape, Jr., "Roman Women in the History of Rhetoric and Oratory," in *Listening to Their Voices*, ed. Molly Meijer Wertheimer (Columbia: University of South Carolina Press, 1997), 117.
75. Cape, "Roman Women in the History of Rhetoric and Oratory," 117–18.

Sermon

1. This sermon was preached at the 2022 St. Olaf Conference on Worship, Theology, and the Arts at St. Olaf College in Northfield, Minnesota. The conference theme was "Scatter the Imagination of Our Hearts," and the audience was Lutheran pastors and church leaders. Scripture Readings are Luke 1:39–45; Genesis 17:15–22; Psalm 78:1–7; Romans 8:18–25 from *A Women's Lectionary for the Whole Church*, Advent 2, by Wilda C. Gafney (New York: Church Publishing Incorporated, 2021), 4–7.
2. "The Magnificat," *All Creation Sings, Evangelical Worship Supplement* (Minneapolis, MN: Augsburg Fortress Press, 2020), Setting 12.
3. Susan Connelly, "The Magnificat as Social Document," 8–11.
4. Leanne B. Simpson, *As We Have Always Done*, 159; Tink Tinker, "Relationship, Not Ownership: Indigenous Lands and Colonial Occupation," *Journal of Tribal Studies* (January 2021): 3.

Bibliography

Adogame, Afe, Raimundo Barreto, and Wanderley P. de Rosa, eds. *Migration and Public Discourse in World Christianity*. Minneapolis. MI: Fortress Press, 2019.
Allen, Ronald, ed. *Preaching the Manifold Grace of God: Theologies of Preaching in the Early Twenty-First Century*. Eugene, OR: Cascade Books, 2022.
———, ed. *Patterns of Preaching: A Sermon Sampler*. St. Louis, MO: Chalice Press, 1998.
Anderson, Herbert and Edward Foley. *Mighty Stories, Dangerous Rituals: Weaving Together the Human and the Divine*. Hoboken, NJ: John Wiley and Sons, 1998.
Augsburger, David. *Pastoral Counseling Across Cultures*. Philadelphia, PA: Westminster Press, 1986.
Augustine. *On Christian Doctrine*. Trans. D. W. Robertson, Jr. New York: MacMillan Publishing Company, 1958.
———. "Sermons on New Testament Lessons." In *Nicene and Post-Nicene Fathers of the Christian Church*. Vol. VI. Philip Schaff, ed. Grand Rapids, MI: William B. Eerdmans Publishing Company, 1979.
Baker, Christopher. *The Hybrid Church in the City: Third Space Thinking*. London: SPM Press, 2009.
Bauman, Zygmunt. *Strangers at Our Door*. Cambridge, UK: Polity Press, 2016.
———. *Liquid Times: Living in an Age of Uncertainty*. Cambridge, UK: Polity Publisher, 2006.
Beaudoin, Tom. "Postmodern Practical Theology." 187–202, in *Opening the Field of Practical Theology: An Introduction*, edited by Kathleen A. Cahalan and Gordon S. Mikoski. Lanham, MD: Rowman & Littlefield, 2014.
Beecher, Henry Ward. *Yale Lectures on Preaching*. New York: J. B. Ford and Company, 1873.
Bhabha, Homi. *The Location of Culture*. New York: Routledge, 1994.
———. "Culture's In-Between." 53–60, in *Questions of Cultural Identity*, edited by Stuart Hall and Paul de Gay. New York: Sage Publications, 1996.
Billman, Kathleen D., and Daniel Migliore. *Rachel's Cry: Prayer of Lament and Rebirth of Hope*. Cleveland, OH: The Pilgrim Press, 1999.

BIBLIOGRAPHY

Boesak, Allan Aubrey, and Curtiss Paul DeYoung. *Radical Reconciliation: Beyond Political Pietism and Christian Quietism*. Maryknoll, NY: Orbis Books, 2018.
Bray, Karen. "Ungrounded Innocence: Confronting Christian Culpability in White Nationalism." 45–52, in *Doing Theology in the Age of Trump: A Critical Report on Christian Nationalism*, edited by Jeffrey W. Robbins and Clayton Crockett. Eugene, OR: Wipf and Stock Publishers, 2018.
British Broadcasting Corporation. "How Many Ukrainian Refugees Are There?" (August 18, 2022).
Browning, Don S. *A Fundamental Practical Theology: Descriptive and Strategic Proposals*. Minneapolis, MN: Fortress Press, 1991.
Brownlee, Annette. *Preaching Jesus Christ Today: Six Questions for Moving from Scripture to Sermon*. Grand Rapids, MI: Baker Academic, 2018.
Bruce, F. F. *The Gospel of John: Introduction, Exposition, and Notes*. Grand Rapids, MI: William B. Eerdmans Publishing Company, 1984.
Brueggemann, Walter. *Tenacious Solidarity: Biblical Provocations on Race, Religion, Climate, and the Economy*. Minneapolis, MN: Fortress Press, 2018.
Burger, Ariel. *Witness: Lessons from Elie Wiesel's Classroom*. San Francisco, CA: HarperOne, 2019.
Buttrick, David. *Preaching Jesus Christ*. 2nd ed. Philadelphia, PA: Fortress Press, 1988.
Cahalan, Kathleen. "Unknowing: Spiritual Practices and the Search for a Wisdom Epistemology." 275–321, in *Christian Practical Wisdom: What It Is, Why It Matters*, coauthored by Dorothy C. Bass, Kathleen A. Cahalan, Bonnie J. Miller-McLemore, James R. Nieman, and Christian B. Scharen. Grand Rapids, MI: William B. Eerdmans Publishing Company, 2016.
Campbell, Charles. *Preaching Jesus: New Directions for Homiletics in Hans Frei's Postliberal Theology*. Grand Rapids, MI: Wm. B. Eerdmans Publishing Company, 1997.
Calvin, John. *Commentary on the Gospel According to John*. Vol. 2. Trans. William Pringle. Grand Rapids, MI: William B. Eerdmans Publishing Company, 1956.
Cannon, Katie. "Christian Imperialism and the Transatlantic Slave Trade." *Journal of Feminist Studies in Religion* 24. no. 1 (2008): 127–34.
Carter, Niambi Michele. *American While Black: African American Immigration and the Limits of Citizenship*. Oxford, UK: Oxford University Press, 2019.
Carter, Warren. *Matthew and the Margins*. Sheffield, England: Sheffield Academic Press, 2000.
———. *John and Empire: Initial Explorations*. New York: T& T Clark, 2008.
Coffin, William Sloane. "The Task Ahead." 177–82, in *Sanctuary: A Resource Guide for Understanding and Participating in the Central American Refugees' Struggle*, edited by Gary Maceoin. New York: HarperCollins, 1985.
Connelly, Susan. "The Magnificat as Social Document." *Compass; Kensington* 48, no. 4 (Summer 2014): 8–11.

Bibliography

Crites, Stephen. "Narrative Quality of Experience." *Journal of the American Academy of Religion* 39, no. 3 (1971): 299.

De la Torre, Miguel. *The U.S. Immigration Crisis: Toward an Ethics of Place*. Eugene, OR: Cascade Books, 2016.

———. "Why I'm Here." 15–24, in *Preaching in/and the Borderlands*, edited by Dwayne Howell and Charles Aaron, Jr. Eugene, OR: Pickwick Publications, 2020.

De la Torre, Vincent. "Trails of Hope and Terror." https://www.trailsofhopeandterrorthemovie.com/buy-the-film.html.

Dube, Musa W. and Jeffrey L. Stanley. *John and Postcolonialism: Travel, Space, and Power*. London: Sheffield Academic Press, 2002.

Elizondo, Virgilio. *Galilean Journey: The Mexican American Promise*. 2nd ed. Maryknoll, NY: Orbis Books, 2005.

Ellithorpe, Anne-Marie. *Towards Friendship-Shaped Communities: A Practical Theology of Friendship*. Oxford, UK: Wiley Blackwell, 2022.

Gundry, Robert H. *Matthew: A Commentary on His Handbook for a Mixed Church under Persecution*. Grand Rapids, MI: William B. Eerdmans Publishing Company, 1982.

Halbwachs, Maurice. *On Collective Memory*. Trans. Lewis A. Coser. Chicago: The University of Chicago Press, 1992.

Hall, Steward, and Paul de Gay. *Questions of Cultural Identity*. New York: Sage Publications. 1996.

Haroutunian, Joseph. *Calvin: Commentaries*. London: SCM Press, 1958.

Horsley, Richard. *Jesus and Empire*. Minneapolis, MN: Augsburg Fortress, 2002.

Howell, Dwayne and Charles Aaron, Jr. eds. *Preaching in/and the Borderlands*. Eugene, OR: Pickwick Publications, 2020.

Isasi-Diaz, Ada Maria. *Mujerista Theology: A Theology for the Twenty-First Century*. Maryknoll, NY: Orbis Press, 1996.

Jagessar, Michael N. & Stephen Burns. *Christian Worship: Postcolonial Perspectives*. Oakville, CT: Equinox Publishing Ltd., 2011.

Jennings, Willie James. *The Christian Imagination: Theology and the Origin of Race*. New Haven, CT: Yale University Press, 2010.

Johnson, Elizabeth. *Truly Our Sister: A Theology of Mary in the Communion of Saints*. New York: Continuum, 2003.

———. "Mary, Mary, Quite Contrary." https://uscatholic.org/articles/201101/mary-mary-quite-contrary/.

Johnson, Mark. *The Body in the Mind: The Bodily Basis of Meaning, Imagination, and Reason*. Chicago: University of Chicago Press, 1987.

Jones, Serene. *Trauma and Grace: Theology in a Ruptured World*. Louisville, KY: Westminster John Knox Press, 2009.

Jones, Timothy. "Black Preaching in Brown Places: Towards the Development of a Black Mestizo Homiletic." *Homiletic* 40, no. 1 (2015): 44.

BIBLIOGRAPHY

Keller, Catherine, Michael Nausner, and Mayra Rivera, eds. *Postcolonial Theologies: Divinity and Empire*. St. Louis, MO: Chalice Press, 2004.
Keller, Catherine. *God and Power: Counter-Apocalyptic Journeys*. Minneapolis, MN: Augsburg Fortress Press, 2005.
Kidwell, Clara, Homer Noley, and George E. "Tink" Tinker. *A Native American Theology*. Maryknoll, NY: Orbis Press, 2001.
Kim, Eunjoo Mary. *Preaching the Presence of God: A Homiletic from an Asian American Perspective*. Valley Forge, PA: Judson Press, 1999.
———. *Women Preaching: Theology and Practice through the Ages*. Cleveland, OH: Pilgrim Press, 2004.
———. *Preaching in an Age of Globalization*. Louisville, KY: Westminster John Knox Press, 2010.
———. *Christian Preaching and Worship in Multicultural Contexts*. Collegeville, MN: Liturgical Press, 2017.
Kim-Cragg, HyeRan. *Postcolonial Preaching: Creating a Ripple Effect*. Lanham, MD: Lexington Books, 2021.
King, Martin Luther, Jr. *Where Do We Go from Here: Chaos or Community?* Boston, MA: Beacon Press, 1968.
Klor de Alva, J. Jorge. "The Postcolonialization of the (Latin) American Experiences: A Reconsideration of 'Colonialism,' 'Postcolonialism,' and 'Mestizaje.'" 241–278, in *After Colonialism: Imperial Histories and Postcolonial Displacements*, edited by Gyan Prakash. Princeton, NJ: Princeton University Press, 1995.
Kwok, Pui-lan. *Postcolonial Imagination and Feminist Theology*. Louisville, KY: Westminster John Knox Press, 2005.
Lee, Sang Hyun. *From a Liminal Place: An Asian American Theology*. Minneapolis, MN: Fortress Press, 2010.
Lehmann, Paul. *Ethics in a Christian Context*. San Francisco, CA: Harper San Francisco, 1976.
Lindas, Barnabas. *The Gospel of John*. Grand Rapids, MI: William B. Eerdmans Publishing Company, 1982.
Loder, James E., and W. Jim Neidhardt. *The Knight's Move: The Relational Logic of the Spirit in Theology and Science*. Colorado Springs, CO: Holmers & Howard Publishers, 1992.
MacIntyre, Alasdair. *After Virtue*. 2nd ed. Notre Dame, IN: University of Notre Dame Press, 1984.
Martinez, Demetria, Alicia Gaspar de Alba, and María Herrera-Sobek. *Three Times a Woman*. Tempe, AZ: Bilingual Review Press, 1989.
Mays, James. *Harper's Bible Commentary*. San Francisco, CA: Harper & Row Publishers, 1988.
McClure, John. *Other-wise Preaching: A Postmodern Ethic for Homiletics*. St. Louis, MO: Chalice Press, 2001.

McFague, Sallie. *Models of God: Theology for an Ecological, Nuclear Age.* Philadelphia, PA: Fortress Press, 1987.
McKeon, Richard, ed. *The Basic Works of Aristotle.* New York: Random House, 1941.
McLoughlin, William G. *Champions of the Cherokees: Evans and John B. Jones.* Princeton, NJ: Princeton University Press, 1990.
Menakem, Resaa. *My Grandmother's Hands: Radicalized Trauma and the Pathway to Mending Our Hearts and Bodies.* Las Vagas, NV: Central Recovery Press, 2022.
Mercer, Joyce Ann. "Feminist and Womanist Practical Theology." 97–114, in *Opening the Field of Practical Theology: An Introduction*, edited by Kathleen A. Cahalan and Gordon S. Mikoski. Lanham, MD: Rowman & Littlefield, 2014.
Metz, Johann Baptist. *Faith in History and Society: Toward a Practical Fundamental Theology.* Freiburg, Germany: Herder and Herder Publishing, 2007.
Min, Ansel. *The Solidarity of Others in a Divided World: A Postmodern Theology after Postmodernism.* New York: T & T Clark International, 2004.
Murry, Shirley and Carlton Young. "Star-Child." #2095 in *The Faith We Sing*, edited by Hoyt L. Hickman. Nashville, TN: Abingdon Press, 2000.
Neuger, Christie C. "Pastoral Counseling as an Art of Personal Political Activism." 88–117, in *The Arts of Ministry: Feminist-Womanist Approaches*, edited by Christie C. Neuger. Louisville, KY: Westminster John Knox Press, 1996.
Newcomb, Steven T. *Pagans in the Promised Land: Decoding the Doctrine of Christian Discovery.* 3rd ed. Chicago: Chicago Review Press, 2008.
Newsom, Carol A., Sharon H. Ringe, and Jacqueline E. Lapsley, eds. *Women's Bible Commentary.* 3rd ed. Louisville, KY: Westminster John Knox Press, 2012.
Osmer, Richard. *Practical Theology: An Introduction.* Grand Rapids, MI: William B. Eerdmans Publishing Company, 2008.
Park, Andrew Sung. *Triune Atonement: Christ's Healing for Sinners, Victims, and the Whole Creation.* Louisville, KY: Westminster John Knox Press, 2009.
Powery, Luke. *Becoming Human: The Holy Spirit and the Rhetoric of Race.* Louisville, KY: Westminster John Knox Press, 2022.
Rabinow, Paul, ed. *The Foucault Reader.* New York: Pantheon Books, 1984.
Rambo, Shelly. *Resurrecting Wounds: Living in the Afterlife of Trauma.* Waco, TX: Baylor University Press, 2017.
Ricoeur, Paul. *Oneself as Another.* Trans. Kathleen Blamey. Chicago: The University of Chicago Press, 1992.
———. *The Course of Recognition.* Trans. David Pellauer. Cambridge, MA: Harvard University Press, 2005.
———. *Interpretation Theory: Discourse and the Surplus of Meaning.* Fort Worth, TX: Texas Christian University Press, 1976.

———. *Memory, History, Forgetting*. Trans. Kathleen Blamey and Davis Pellauer. Chicago: The University of Chicago Press, 2004.

Rieger, Joerg. *Christ & Empire: From Paul to Postcolonial Times*. Minneapolis, MN: Fortress Press, 2007.

———. *Theology in the Capitalocene: Ecology, Identity, Class, and Solidarity*. Minneapolis, MN: Fortress Press, 2022.

Rivera, Mayra. *The Touch of Transcendence: A Postcolonial Theology of God*. Louisville, KY: Westminster John Knox Press, 2007.

Robbins, Jefferey W. and Clayton Crockett. *Doing Theology in the Age of Trump: A Critical Report on Christian Nationalism*. Eugene, OR: Wipf and Stock Publishers, 2018.

Robert, Dana. *Faithful Friendships: Embracing Diversity in Christian Community*. Grand Rapids, MI: William B. Eerdmans Publishing Company, 2019.

Russell, Letty. *Just Hospitality: God's Welcome in a World of Difference*. Louisville, KY: Westminster John Knox Press, 2009.

Sacks, Jonathan. "The Chief Rabbi's New Year Message." BBC Online Religion & Ethics (2001). http://www.chiefrabbi.org/articles/other/rhbbc.htm (December 18, 2021).

Said, Edward. *Culture and Imperialism*. New York: Vantage House, 1994.

———. "Secular Interpretation, the Geographical Element, and the Methodology of Imperialism." 21–39 in *After Colonialism: Imperial Histories and Postcolonial Displacements*, edited by Gyan Prakash. Princeton, NJ: Princeton University Press, 1995.

Schaberg, Jane. *The Illegitimacy of Jesus: A Feminist Theological Interpretation of the Infancy Narrative*. New York: HarperCollins, 1987.

Segovia, Fernando F., and Mary Ann Tolbert (eds.). *Teaching the Bible: The Discourses and Politics of Biblical Pedagogy*. Maryknoll, NY: Orbis Books, 1998.

Sherry, Patrick. *Spirit and Beauty: An Introduction to Theological Aesthetics*. 2nd ed. London: SCM Press, 2002.

Simpson, Leanne B. *As We Have Always Done: Indigenous Freedom through Radical Resistance*. Minneapolis: University of Minnesota Press, 2020.

Smith, Mitzi, and Jayachitra Lalitha, eds. *Teaching All Nations: Interrogating the Matthean Great Commission*. Minneapolis, MN: Fortress Press, 2014.

Spillers, Hortense J. *Black, White, and in Color: Essays on American Literature and Culture*. Chicago: The University of Chicago Press, 2003.

Sugirtharaja, R. S. *Postcolonial Criticism and Biblical Interpretation*. New York: Oxford University Press, 2002.

———, ed. *Voices from the Margin: Interpreting the Bible in the Third World*. Maryknoll, NY: Obis Books. 1997.

Talley, Thomas. *The Origins of the Liturgical Year*. 2nd ed. Collegeville, MN: Liturgical Press, 1991.

Tanner, Kathryn. *Theories of Culture: A New Agenda for Theology*. Minneapolis, MN: Fortress Press, 1997.

Bibliography

Tinker, George "Tink." "Relationship, Not Ownership: Indigenous Lands and Colonial Occupation." Unpublished.

Travis, Sarah. *Decolonizing Preaching: The Pulpit as Postcolonial Space*. Eugene, OR: Cascade Books, 2014.

———. *Unspeakable: Preaching and Trauma-Informed Theology*. Eugene, OR: Cascade Books, 2021.

UNHCR. https://www.unrefugees.org/refugee-facts/ (August 18, 2022).

Volf, Miroslav. *The End of Memory: Remembering Rightly in a Violent World*. Grand Rapids, MI: William B. Eerdmans Publishing Company, 2006.

Wagman, Herman. *Christian Worship in East and West: A Study Guide to Liturgical History*. Trans. Gordon W. Lathrop. Collegeville, MN: Liturgical Press, 1985.

Walker, Williston, Richard A. Norris, David W. Lotz, and Robert T. Handy. *A History of the Christian Church*. 4th ed. New York: Charles Scribner's Sons, 1985.

Ware, Corrine. *Discover Your Spiritual Type: A Guide to Individual and Congregational Growth*. Lanham, MD: Rowman & Littlefield. 1995.

Wertheimer, Molly M. (ed.). *Listening to Their Voices*. Columbia: University of South Carolina Press, 1997.

Whyte, Kyle. "Critical Investigations of Resilience: A Brief Introduction to Indigenous Environmental Studies and Sciences." *Daedalus: Journal of the American Academy of Arts and Sciences* 147, no. 2 (Spring 2018): 137.

Willimon, Willam H., and Richard Lischer. *Concise Encyclopedia of Preaching*. Louisville, KY: Westminster/John Knox, 1995.

Wilson, Paul S. *Imagination of the Heart: New Understandings in Preaching*. Nashville, TN: Abingdon Press, 1988.

Winn, Adam, ed. *An Introduction to Empire in the New Testament*. Atlanta, GA: SBL Press, 2016.

Woodly, Randy. *Indigenous Theology and the Western Worldview: A Decolonized Approach to Christian Doctrine*. Grand Rapids, MI: Baker Academic, 2022.

Wymer, Andrew. "Betraying White Preaching: 'Responsible' and 'Realistic' White Preaching." The 2019 Academy of Homiletics Workgroup Papers.257. https://d2r0txsugik6oi.cloudfront.net/neon/resource/academyofhomiletics/files/2019%20AOH%20Workgroup%20Papers%20Final.pdf.

Wymer, Andrew and Lis Valle-Ruiz, *Unmasking White Preaching: Racial Hegemony, Resistance, and Possibilities in Homiletics*. Lanham, MD: Lexington Books, 2022.

———. "Betraying White Preaching: 'Responsible' and 'Realistic' White Preaching." Paper presented at the annual meeting of the Academy of Homiletics, Princeton, NJ, December 2019. https://d2r0txsugik6oi.cloudfront.net/neon/resource/academyofhomiletics/files/2019%20AOH%20Workgroup%20Papers%20Final.pdf

Index

Academy of Homiletics, 7
Acts, Chapter 2, 94
adultery, 31
Africa, 81
African American people, 59–60, 70–71
Alexander VI (Pope), 81
American citizens, privilege of, 38
American colonialism, 49
American Exceptionalism, 69–70
amnesia, 56
analogical imagination, 65
Anderson, Herbert, 55
Argentina, 36, 105–6
argument (*contentio*), 98–99
Arianism, 62
Aristotle, 21, 92
art, 22, 57–58
Ash Wednesday, 12, 113n35
Asian American women, sexism relation to, 14–15
atonement, 63
Augsburger, David, 77
Augustine (Saint), 6, 63

authority, of Jesus, 12, 88

Babylonian Empire, 49–50
baptism, 89–90; *koinonia* of, 93
Barth, xi
Bauman, Zygmunt, 52
Beaudoin, Tom, 9–10
Beecher Lectures, at Yale Divinity School, ix
Bethlehem, 45
Bhabha, Homi, 8
the Bible, x, 25, 59, 85; cultural intertextuality and, 65; intertextuality in, 87, 88–89; personal conversation in, 98; postcolonial self in, 11–12; strangers in, 43
Black bodies, 70–71
bodily presence, of Jesus: reconciliation relation to, 75; resurrection as, 67
The Body in the Mind (Johnson, M.), 22
boundaries, 16–17, 18, 20
Bray, Karen, 23
Brownlee, Annette, 2

Brueggemann, Walter, 56
Buddhism, 97–98, 122n38
Buddhist mission, 87, 89, 90
Bultmann, Rudolf, xi
Burger, Ariel, 52
Burns, Stephen, 44
Buttrick, David, 2, 43

Calvin, John, 60–62, 63
Cambridge, England, 44
Campbell, Charles, 2, 25–26
Cannon, Katie, 80, 81–82
capitalism, neoliberal, 92
Caribbean basin, 47
Carter, Niambi Michele, 49, 53
Carter, Warren, 46, 65–66, 67, 68, 119n24; on Great Commission, 85–86
Chang Sang, xi
children, 49, 54, 58
Chimayó, New Mexico, 117n15
Chinese sages, 92
Christian identity, 7, 25–26; postcolonial imagination relation to, 28
"Christian Imperialism and the Transatlantic Slave Trade" (Cannon), 80
Christianity, 61; colonialism relation to, 70, 79; Indigenous peoples relation to, 82–83; Roman Empire relation to, 62–63
Christian Preaching and Worship in Multicultural Contexts (Kim), xii
Christmas, 57–58
Christology, European, 27–28
Church Dogmatics (Barth), xi
Cicero, 92, 98–99
Clay, Henry, 69–70
Coffin, William Sloane, 46
colonial imagination, 23, 33–34, 38; identity in, 37
colonialism, xiii, 2–3, 38, 44, 54, 107; Christianity relation to, 70, 79; economic disparity and, x; European, 1, 6; freedom relation to, 35–36; Great Commission relation to, 80, 88; hospitality relation to, 56–57; missionaries and, 82–83; otherness and, 11; preachers relation to, 95–96; reconciliation relation to, 72; trauma of, 69; violence of, 65
the colonized, xiii, xiv, 8, 41, 59, 77–78; the colonizer relation to, 33; forgiveness by, 76; identity of, 13; marginalization of, 5, 69; memories of, 71–72; postcolonial imagination,

24; preachers relation to, 27, 75; reconciliation and, 74; Samaritan woman as, 18; stories of, 19; suffering of, 46, 50–52, 83, 93; voices of, 45
the colonizer, xiii, 2, 24, 74, 76; the colonized relation to, 33; forgiveness of, 67, 93
communication, 37, 97
communion (*koinonia*), 93
community: baptism and, 90; of friendship, 93–95, 98; Great Commission relation to, 96–97; identity of, 2
community letter, 38–39, 101–10
Confucianism, 92, 97–98
congregational songs, in preaching, 19
Constantine I (Emperor), 62–63
contentio (argument), 98–99
contrapuntal music, 17–18, 76–77
conversation, 97–99. *See also sermo*
conversion, of Paul, the Apostle, 95
Council of Chalcedon, 62–63
counter memory, 69, 75
COVID-19 pandemic, 48–49
Crites, Stephen, 19
crucifixion, 63, 64, 119n14

cryptic riddles, 97–98
cultural intertextuality, the Bible and, 65
cultural justice, 34
culture, 94–95; European American Puritan, 23; Jewish, 2; patriarchal colonial, 29; Western, 4–5, 92–93
Culture and Imperialism (Said), 17

Daniel, Chapter 7, 89
Deborah, 35
Decolonizing Preaching (Travis), x, 6–7
De Doctrina Christiana (St. Augustine), 6
De la Torre, Miguel, 56–57
De la Torre, Vincent, 57
destruction: of ecosystem, 33–34; imperialism and, 55
Deuteronomy, Chapter 33, 89
DeYoung, Curtis Paul, 72, 74
dialectical communication, 37
dialogical imagination, 24
dialogue, 18–19, 97; with strangers, 85
diasporic imagination, 24–25
discernment, rational, 21
disciples, 90–91, 110
discipline, spiritual, 26
discrimination, 14
diseases, 69

Doctrine of Discovery, 69–70, 81
domination, 59, 83–84; of Indigenous peoples, 80–81
doubt, of Thomas, 61, 89
Dube, Musa W., 12–13, 14, 79, 86–87

Easter, 12, 29, 59; imperialism and, 63–64; preachers on, 61; reconciliation and, 78
economic disparity: colonial imagination and, 33–34; colonialism and, x; in US, 96
economic justice, 34, 42
ecosystem, destruction of, 33–34
Edwards, Jonathan, 70
Egypt, xv, 41, 43, 45, 52–53
Elizabeth, 28; community letter to, 38–39, 101–10; Holy Spirit relation to, 31–32; Mary and, 106, 108–9; in postcolonial imagination, 29; pregnancy of, 30, 102, 103
Elizondo, Virgilio, 49
Ellithorpe, Anne-Marie, 92
empathy, 77
The End of Memory (Volf), 35
enlightenment, 63, 88
environmental justice, 34
eternal life, 67–68
European American Protestant churches, 44
European American Puritan culture, 23
European Christology, 27–28
European colonialism, 1, 6
Ewha Woman's University, xi
extratextuality, 87

faith, 52, 61, 68
Faith in History and Society (Metz), 54
farewell discourse, 89
"Feast of Annunciation," 28
"Feast of the Ever-Blessed Virgin Mary," 28–29
Feast of the Holy Innocents, 44
feminist theology, 12
"Festival of Lessons and Carols," 44
Foley, Edward, 55
foreigner syndrome, 14
forgiveness, 74; by the colonized, 76; of the colonizer, 67, 93; resurrection relation to, 72–73
Foucault, Michel, 69
freedom, 35–36, 62, 90
Frei, Hans, 25
friendship, 80, 92; community of, 93–95, 98; freedom relation to, 90; meta

preaching for, 97;
missionaries relation to, 91;
in personal conversation, 99;
for reconciliation, 96

Gabriel, 28, 30
Gafney, Wilda, 28–29
The Galilean Journey (Elizondo), 49
Galilee, Roman soldiers in, 30–31
Genesis, 93
genocide, of Native American people, 70
globalization, *kairos* of, 3
God, 21, 26, 31, 52, 54, 55; Son of, 53, 60, 61, 62, 119n14; Triune, xiv, 1, 86, 93
Goodell, William, 70
Great Commission, of Jesus, xv, 69–70, 85–86, 92; colonialism relation to, 80, 88; community relation to, 96–97; imperialism relation to, 79, 84; intertextuality in, 88–89, 91; missionaries relation to, 87, 95; white supremacy relation to, 81, 82–83
Gregory, the Great, 113n35
Guatemala, 36, 106

Halbwachs, Maurice, 66

Hannah, 35
healing, reconciliation and, 58, 64, 67, 68
Herod (King), 45, 49, 52
historical imagination, 24
Holy Spirit, 26, 78; Elizabeth relation to, 31–32; forgiveness relation to, 73–74; Mary relation to, 30; reconciliation relation to, 77; in third space, 27, 32; transformation and, 76
Holy Trinity, 62
Homiletic (journal), 7
homiletics, x–xi, xii, 1, 6, 7
hope, 52, 53, 55, 58
Horsley, Richard, 64
hospitality, 56–57
Hughes, Charles Evans, 46–47
humanization, 78
human spirit, 26
hybridity, 8, 9, 10
Hyuk Huh, xi

identity, 10–11; Christian, 7, 25–26, 28; in colonial imagination, 37; of the colonized, 13; of community, 2; of disciples, 90–91; of Jesus, xiii, xiv, 1, 6, 8, 27, 34–35, 41, 53, 54; Lent relation to, 12; mutual recognition of, 16; postcolonial, 13–14, 18;

of preachers, 95–96; of reconciliation, 75–76; of Samaritan woman, 17; of superiority, 74; in third space, 9; transformation of, 19–20; white supremacy in, 5–6

The Illegitimacy of Jesus (Schaberg), 30

images, 21–22; of Jesus, 18, 25, 42, 84

"Images of Jesus in Advancing the Great Commission" (Winborne), 84

imagination, 21, 24–25, 110; analogical, 65; colonial, 23, 33–34, 37, 38; God relation to, 26; reason relation to, 22–23. *See also* postcolonial imagination

immigration, 14, 56. *See also* migrants

immigration policy, 52

imperialism, xiv–xv, 8, 14, 36, 108; colonialism and, x; destruction and, 55; Easter and, 63–64; Gospel of John relation to, 59; Gospel of Matthew relation to, 86; Great Commission relation to, 79, 84; Jews relation to, 68; patriarchy and, 13; reconciliation relation to, 72; of Roman Empire, 15; suffering and, 46; trauma of, 69; in US, 96; violence of, 67; Western, xii, 3–5

Indian Anglican churches, 36, 105

Indigenous peoples, 80–83. *See also* Native American people

interpathy, for third space, 77

interpretation, of questions, 29

intertextuality, 87, 119n24; in Great Commission, 88–89, 91

Isaiah, 35

Jagessar, Michael, 44
Japan, xi
Jennings, Willie James, 23, 72
Jeremiah, 45, 49–50
Jesus. *See specific topics*
Jesus Movement, 86
Jewish culture, 2
Jews, 29–30; imperialism relation to, 68; Samaritans relation to, 13, 16
Jim Crow laws, 71
John, Gospel of, 67–68, 89; Chapter 4, xiv, 12, 15–16; Chapter 20, xv, 59, 63, 64, 65–66, 72; resurrection in, 60
Johnson, Elizabeth, 32
Johnson, Mark, 22
Jones, Serene, 117n12
Joseph, 31, 45, 49, 52–53

Judith, 35
Just Hospitality (Russell), 5, 56
justice, 34, 52, 59
juxtaposition, 87

kairos, of globalization, 3
Keller, Catherine, 8
Kim-Cragg, HyeRan, x, 7
King, Martin Luther, Jr., 96
King's College, Cambridge, 44
koinonia (communion), 93
Korea, xi
The Korean War, xi
Kuyper, Abraham, 82–83
Kwang-sun Suh, David, xi
Kwok Pui-lan, 3, 24–26, 87

Latin Americans, 46–49, 57
Lent, 12, 28, 113n35
Leo I (Pope), 63
Leviticus, 43
liberation, 4–5, 12; in the Bible, 59; from superiority, 74
Lindbeck, George, 25
The Location of Culture (Bhabha), 8
Lose, David, 2
Louisville Institute, Sabbatical Research Grant of, ix
Luke, Gospel of, xiv, 22, 28, 31, 35, 89; personal conversation in, 98

Magdalene, Mary, 60, 61, 64–65, 67
"The Magnificat," 28, 104–5
Mahavagga, 87–88
Manifest Destiny, 46, 69–70
manipulative speech, 99
Marcian (Emperor), 63
marginalization, 5, 15, 69
Martinez, Demetria, 47–48
Mary, xiv, 49, 117n12; community letter to, 38–39, 101–10; Elizabeth and, 106, 108–9; Holy Spirit relation to, 30; Joseph and, 45; pregnancy of, 28, 29, 31–32, 101, 102–3; song of, 22, 32–37, 104–5, 110
Matthew, Gospel of, xv, 41, 49–50, 52, 85–86, 88; Chapter 28, 79, 80, 93; disciples in, 90; Mary in, 31. *See also* Great Commission, of Jesus
McClure, John, 69
McLean, Robert, 83–84
memories, 54–55, 69, 119n26; of the colonized, 71–72; in Gospel of John, 66; imagination and, 23–24
Menakem, Resmaa, 71
Mercer, Joyce Ann, xiv
Messiah, 1, 16
meta preaching, 80, 97–99
Metz, Johann Baptist, 54

Middle Passage, 70
Mighty Stories, Dangerous Rituals (Anderson and Foley), 55
migrants, 49, 54, 56–57, 96; Joseph as, 52–53; at US-Mexico border, 47
Min, Ansel, 3
Minnesota, Northfield, 124n1
Miriam, 35
missio Dei (mission of God), 91
missionaries, 91; colonialism and, 82–83; Great Commission relation to, 87, 95; white supremacy relation to, 92
"mission of God." *See missio Dei*
model minority stereotype, 14
Moses, 89
"Mothers of the Disappeared," 36, 105–6
mourning, 77, 78
Murry, Shirley, 58
music, contrapuntal, 17–18, 76–77
mutual recognition, of identity, 16
Myers, Ched, 46
myths, 25

narrative preaching, 37

Native American people, 22, 33–34, 69–70, 74, 108; freedom relation to, 35–36; reconciliation for, 59–60
Nativity stories, 41, 43
neocolonialism, x, 3, 41–42; otherness and, 11; preachers relation to, 95–96. *See also* colonialism
neoliberal capitalism, 92
New Homiletic, 37
New Mexico, Chimayó, 117n15
Nicaragua, 46–47
Northfield, Minnesota, 124n1

Oneself as Another (Ricoeur), 10–11
"Only Say the Word" (Martinez), 47–48, 50–51, 57
optative mood, 76–77
Osmer, Richard, 29
otherness, 96; postcolonial self relation to, 11–12; transformation and, 95

Pali Canon, 87–88, 122n38
Park Soon-Kyung, xi
Parousia, 81
patriarchal colonial culture, 29
patriarchy, 13, 29–31, 45, 103–4
Paul, the Apostle, 89–90, 95

Pax Americana, 45–47, 54, 56, 66; privilege in, 55, 58
Pax Romana, 45–46, 66
PCSD. *See* post-colonial stress disorder
penitential observance, 12
Pentecost, 29
personal conversation, 97–98
philosophical phenomenology, 11
phronesis, 21
political refugee, Jesus as, 41, 43–44, 52, 54
Portugal, 81
postcolonial identity, 13–14, 18
postcolonial imagination, 23–25, 34, 38–39, 45–46; of Gospel of John, 66–67; Mary in, 28, 29, 31–32, 33; preachers relation to, 26–28
Postcolonial Imagination and Feminist Theology (Kwok), 3
postcolonialism. *See specific topics*
Postcolonial Preaching (HyeRan), 7
Postcolonial Preaching (Kim-Cragg), x
postcolonial self, 11–12, 17, 18, 20, 27
post-colonial stress disorder (PCSD), 70
post-traumatic stress disorder (PTSD), 71
poverty, 107
the power of oratory (*vis ortionis*), 98–99
Practical Theology (Osmer), 29
prayer, 39, 77; of Native American people, 74
preachers, ix, xv; the colonized relation to, 27, 75; dialogue with, 19; on Easter, 61; identity of, 95–96; postcolonial imagination relation to, 26–28
preaching. *See specific topics*
Preaching in the Age of Globalization (Kim), xii
Preaching Jesus (Campbell), 2
Preaching Jesus (Lose), 2
Preaching Jesus Christ (Buttrick), 2, 43
Preaching Jesus Christ Today (Brownlee), 2
Preaching the Presence of God (Kim), xii
pregnancy: of Elizabeth, 30, 102, 103; of Mary, 28, 29, 31–32, 101, 102–3
Princeton Theological Seminary, xii
privilege, 36, 38, 54, 61, 74; in *Pax Americana*, 55, 58
Protestants, 3, 44, 61
PTSD. *See* post-traumatic stress disorder

Public Religion Research Institute, 56
Puerto Rico, 83–84

questions, 27, 29

"Rachel's cry," 45, 50–51
racism, 14, 42, 96; colonialism and, x
Rambo, Shelly, 60
rational discernment, 21
reason, imagination relation to, 22–23
reconciliation, 55, 57, 59–60; bodily presence relation to, 75; the colonized and, 74; Easter and, 78; friendship for, 96; healing and, 58, 64, 67, 68; Holy Spirit relation to, 77; identity of, 75–76; resurrection relation to, 72–73
Reformation, 63
refugees, 42, 53; political, 41, 43–44, 52, 54
resistance, preaching relation to, 55
resurrection, 60, 63, 67; reconciliation relation to, 72–73
Revised Common Lectionary, 12, 43–44, 60, 80
Ricoeur, Paul, 10–11, 53, 73–74, 76, 119n26

Rieger, Joerg, 37
Rivera, Mayra, 83
Robert, Dana, 92
Roman Catholicism, 62
Roman Empire, 2, 6, 38, 41, 66, 107; Christianity relation to, 62–63; imperialism of, 15; Jesus Movement relation to, 86; taxes of, 32; US compared to, 46; violence of, 64, 90, 117n12
Roman soldiers, in Galilee, 30–31
Russell, Letty, xii, 5, 54, 56
Russia, 42

Sabbatical Research Grant, of Louisville Institute, ix
Sack, Jonathan, 43
Said, Edward, 8, 17
Sallman, Warner, 84
salvation, 52, 61
Samaritans, 13, 15, 16
Samaritan woman, xiv, 1, 15–16, 98; as the colonized, 18; identity of, 17; as postcolonial self, 12; transformation of, 13
Schaberg, Jane, 30
self, postcolonial, 11–12, 17, 18, 20, 27
sermo (conversation), 98–99
sexism, x, xii, 14–15, 42

sexual violence, 30–31
Sherry, Patrick, 22–23
Simpson, Leanne, 34, 35, 36–37
sisterhood, 29
Soares-Probhu, George M., 87–88
solidarity, x, 3, 72, 95; third space for, 5, 36–37
song, of Mary, 22, 28, 32–37, 104–5, 110
Son of God, 53, 60, 61, 62, 119n14
South Korea, xi
Spain, 81
Spillers, Hortense J., 70–71
spirit, 26. *See also* Holy Spirit
Spirit and Beauty (Sherry), 22–23
spiritual discipline, 26
"Star-Child," 57–58
Sterling, Gregory, ix
St. Olaf Conference, 110, 124n1
stories, 25, 41, 43; of the colonized, 19
strangers, 56; in the Bible, 43; dialogue with, 85; meta preaching and, 97; refugees as, 52
suffering, 77, 78, 108; of the colonized, 46, 50–52, 83, 93
superiority, 4–5, 44, 74, 84. *See also* white supremacy

Synoptic Gospels, 15
systemic racism, 14

Tanner, Kathryn, 25
"The Task Ahead" (Coffin), 46
taxes, of Roman Empire, 32
Tenacious Solidarity (Brueggemann), 56
terrorism, 69–70
Theories of Culture (Tanner), 25
third space, 8–9, 18–20, 75–76, 77; Holy Spirit in, 27, 32; postcolonial imagination relation to, 28; for solidarity, 5, 36–37
Thomas, 60, 63, 64–65, 67, 68; doubt of, 61, 89
three-point-and-a-poem lecture style, 19, 37
Thurman, Howard, 27
Tinker, Tink, 33
tokenism, 14
Torontle, Mositi, 13
"Trails of Hope and Terror" (documentary), 57
transatlantic slave trade, 81
transfiguration, 66–67
transformation, x, 3; Holy Spirit and, 76; of identity, 19–20; otherness and, 95; of Samaritan woman, 13
trauma, 64–65, 69; of African American people, 70–71

Trauma and Grace (Jones), 117n12
Travis, Sarah, x, 6–7, 76–77
Treaty of Tordesillas, 81
The Trinity, 93
Trinity Sunday, 80
Triune God, xiv, 1, 86, 93

Ukraine, 42
"Ungrounded Innocence" (Bray), 23
UN High Commissioner for Refugees (UNHCR), 42
United States (US), 49, 83–84, 96; immigration to, 56; Roman Empire compared to, 46
US-Mexico border, 42, 47, 49, 54

Vanderbilt Divinity School, ix
verse-by-verse expository preaching, 37
The Victims (Torontle), 13
Vinaya texts, 87–88
violence, 30–31, 55, 108; of colonialism, 65; of imperialism, 67; of Roman Empire, 64, 90, 117n12
vis ortionis (the power of oratory), 98–99
voices, of the colonized, 45
Volf, Miroslav, 35

War on Drugs, 71
Wegman, Herman, 113n35
Western culture, 4–5, 92–93
Western imperialism, xii, 3–5
White European superiority, 44
white Jesus, 84
whiteness, 6, 23, 84
white supremacy, xii, 6, 9–10, 23, 92, 96; Great Commission relation to, 81, 82–83; hospitality relation to, 56; Western imperialism relation to, 4–5
Whyte, Kyle, 33–34
Winborne, Sheila, 84
wisdom, 21, 26
Witness (Burger), 52
women, voices of, 45
Women Preaching (Kim), xii
A Women's Lectionary for The Whole Church (Gafney), 28–29
Woodley, Randy, 70, 74
Wymer, Andrew, 6

Yale Divinity School, Beecher Lectures at, ix
Young, Carlton, 58

Zacchaeus, 98

About the Author

Eunjoo Mary Kim is the Charles G. Finney Chair, Professor of Homiletics and Liturgics at Vanderbilt University Divinity School. Among her many publications are *Preaching the Presence of God: A Homiletic from an Asian American Perspective*, *Women Preaching: Theology and Practice through the Ages*, *Preaching in an Age of Globalization*, and *Christian Preaching and Worship in Multicultural Contexts*. Kim was the president of the Academy of Homiletics in 2018.

www.ingramcontent.com/pod-product-compliance
Lightning Source LLC
Chambersburg PA
CBHW020053170426
43199CB00009B/270